Audrey Grant's
BETTER BRIDGE

♠ ♥ ♦ ♣ ♠ ♥ ♦ ♣ ♠ ♥ ♦ ♣ ♠ ♥ ♦ ♣ ♠ ♥ ♦ ♣ ♠ ♥ ♦ ♣ ♠

Basics

CP

CENTENNIAL PRESS

ISBN 0–8220–1665–6

Design and composition by
John Reinhardt Book Design

Centennial Press
Box 82087, Lincoln, Nebraska 68501
an imprint of Cliffs Notes, Inc.

♠ ♥ ♦ ♣

To all my students.
Your limitless enthusiasm has made teaching an ongoing adven-
ture. After each class, I've always been able to sincerely say,
"Thank you, I've learned a lot."

Contents

Preface

For many years, I've seen people of all ages and all walks of life playing bridge. These bridge players are so obviously enjoying themselves that I've made it part of my life's work to teach and write about the game.

The best theorists in the world have shared their secrets with me, and I bring these pieces of bridge wisdom to you in a manner which I hope you will find readable.

Bridge is more than a game. It's a wonderful life skill. It's given me—as it can you—friends around the world. Anywhere you travel, being able to play a hand of bridge opens the door to meeting new people.

Here's more good news about bridge. It's healthy. The days of smoke-filled rooms of bridge players are long gone. It's accepted now that bridge exercises the mind the same way that physical activity exercises your body. That's right. Research indicates that the brain actually changes in response to the stimulus which a game like bridge provides.

This first book introduces you to the basics of bidding, play, and defense—the three parts of the game. It will get you started. Once you have played for a while, you will want to add the next three books to your library, which cover each aspect in more detail.

This is a wonderful hobby, and when someone asks if you play bridge, you want to be able to answer yes with confidence.

For me, bridge is a game of friendship and laughter. I'm glad you have decided to become a part of the bridge family.

Audrey Grant

Acknowledgments

To my husband, David Lindop, who works hand-in-hand with me in all my bridge endeavors. Without his talent, drive, and love, these books would still be in the conceptual stage.

To my mother, Connie, who became an expert in counting up to thirteen while making sure every card was in its place.

To my dad, Alex, who writes my bridge jokes—and that's no laughing matter.

To my children, Joanna and Jason, who get involved in so many aspects of the projects—from making crepes for the bridge students to dressing up as cards.

To my brother, Brian, who has helped test much of the material used throughout this series.

To Julie Greenberg, head of the Education Department at the American Contract Bridge League, for her friendship and inspiration, and to the members of her staff for sharing their knowledge about bridge instruction.

To Henry Francis, editor of the *American Contract Bridge League Bulletin*, and his staff, who have been editing my work for years and have helped turn me into a better writer.

To Jerry Helms, the true bridge professional, who has generously shared both his teaching methods and expertise.

To Pat Harrington, whose understanding of the beginners' point of view has helped me write with more clarity to the books.

To Eric Rodwell and Zia Mahmood, world-class players, who have spent countless hours sharing their theories about the game.

To Fred Gitelman and Sheri Winestock, for showing what bridge will look like in the 21st Century.

To Michael Laughlin and Kirk Frederick, for their belief in me, together with their creative input.

To Flip Wilson, for his confidence that even my wildest promotional ideas would work out.

To the American Contract Bridge League Board of Directors, who help provide an overview of how bridge is played in all parts of the country.

To Doug Lincoln, for his vision and his ongoing support of this project.

To Jim Borthwick, who took care of all the details to bring this series to fruition.

To Michele Spence, for the many hours spent proof-reading each page of the manuscript and her cheerful disposition throughout the project.

To John Reinhardt, for combining his bridge knowledge and design talents to make each book in the series pleasing to the eye.

And of course, I'd like to acknowledge all those students, teachers, and expert players who have constantly provided inspiration and ideas in the field of bridge.

Getting Started

> *"You're nothing but a pack of cards!"*
> —Lewis Carroll,
> *Alice's Adventures in Wonderland*

Bridge is one of the most challenging card games in the world. It does, however, have a reputation for being difficult to learn. I'd like to prove otherwise.

If I were teaching you how to play golf or how to play an instrument, I'd expect you to have the necessary equipment. You'd need a golf club for the golf lesson and an instrument for the music lesson. To learn to play bridge, you also need equipment. To get started, you need a *deck* of cards.

The Equipment

Open up your deck of cards and take out the *jokers;* the only jokers at a bridge table are the players having fun. Before going any further, take a few minutes to examine the deck. There are fifty-two cards, divided into four *suits:* spades (♠), hearts (♥), diamonds (♦), and clubs (♣). Two of the suits are black and two are red. Each suit has thirteen cards. The cards in each suit are made up of the numbers from two to ten, and the ace, along with three *face cards*—the king, queen, and jack.

Different card games use all or part of the deck and give importance to certain cards. Some games use the whole deck; others use half the deck. Some designate the jacks as the highest cards in the deck. Bridge uses all fifty-two cards, and the cards in each suit are *ranked* with the ace being the highest, followed by the king, queen, jack, ten—down to the two.

Order of rank—Ace is highest, two is lowest

The top five cards in each suit—the ace, king, queen, jack, and ten—are called the *honors*. The top four cards—the ace, king, queen, and jack—are referred to as the *high cards*. When I have my students lay out the high cards on the table, we give them a round of applause. If, while you're reading this book, you're putting the cards out on a table in your public library, you may not want to do this.

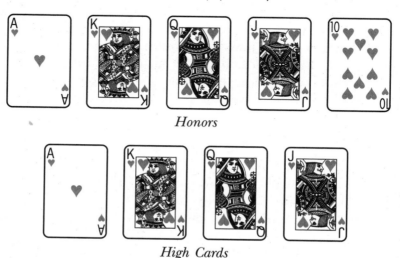

Honors

High Cards

In addition to the cards being ranked from the ace down to the two, the suits are given a ranking. They're ranked in alphabetical order, with Clubs ♣ as the lowest-ranking suit, then Diamonds ♦, Hearts ♥, and finally Spades ♠ as the highest-ranking suit.

♠ **Spades**
♥ **Hearts**   } Major Suits

♦ **Diamonds**
♣ **Clubs**   } Minor Suits

The hearts and spades are referred to as the *major suits*. Clubs and diamonds are referred to as the *minor suits*. As the game unfolds, you'll see why the major suits are more important than the minor suits.

The Players

Bridge is a game played by four people. My friends tried to teach me to play, unsuccessfully, and ended up giving me a large bridge book. I had little experience with any card game at the time and needed to visualize how bridge was played. I got out my deck of cards and went one step further. I set up a table in the corner of the den for a unique game of bridge. There are four players in a bridge game. I sat in one chair, and a stuffed animal sat in each of the three unoccupied chairs. Bridge players are sensitive, so I'd suggest that, if you decide to learn this way, you don't tell anyone you play bridge with animals.

The players are often referred to using compass *directions*. If you look in a bridge book or at the bridge column in a newspaper, you'll see North, South, East, and West used to identify the four players.

Bridge is a *partnership* game. The two players sitting North and South form one partnership, and the two players sitting East and West form the other partnership.

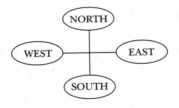

A square table is ideal for a game of bridge; in fact, any arrangement where the four people can face each other in partnerships will work. You may notice bridge being played on trains, buses, planes, or in the park. Not only is the game popular, it's easy to set up.

Watching a Game

Omar Sharif, a great film star and avid bridge player, has said that bridge is a passport to the world. Whether you're traveling in your own neighborhood or around the world, you can have instant friends. You and I could go to London, England, and have tea in the quaint Brown's Hotel. Look, over there, in front of the leaded-glass windows. Isn't that four people about to play cards? Maybe they're going to play bridge.

Let's go closer.

"Hello. We were about to go in for tea when we noticed your bridge game. Would you mind if we watched for a moment?"

"That would be fine," comes the reply, almost simultaneously from the four players. Bridge players rarely mind having someone watch, or *kibitz*, their game, but it's good manners to ask first.

When you kibitz a game of bridge, watch only one player at a time. We'll refer to the four players as North, South, East and West. We can watch the action by looking at South's hand.

Most card games start by *dealing* out the cards, and bridge is no exception. North *shuffles* the cards and then passes the deck to West, the player on the right, who *cuts* the deck in two. North completes the cut by picking up what used to be the bottom half of the deck and placing it on the top. North now starts to deal out the cards in a clockwise direction, face down. In bridge, all of the cards are distributed to the players. At the end of the deal, each player has one quarter of the deck—thirteen cards. The thirteen cards in front of a player are referred to as a *hand.*

South picks up the hand and fans out the cards so that none of the other players at the table can see them; that's part of the game. South sorts the cards into suits, alternating between red and black, placing the high cards in each suit on the left.

You can sort your cards in any manner you please. I like to sort them as South has done. It seems easier for me to remember the cards when they're sorted this way.

Although a bridge hand is held as shown above, for the purpose of representing the hand in a newspaper or a book, the following format is used:

♠ A Q J 8 3
♥ 9 5 4
♦ A K 6
♣ 5 2

The suits are placed in order of rank with spades, the highest-ranking, at the top. "A" represents the ace, "K" the king, "Q" the queen, and "J" the jack.

Back to our game. After all the players have sorted their hands, North, South's partner, says, "One Club."

There are two stages to the game. First, there's an *auction* in which the players *bid* for the privilege of naming a *contract*. This is followed by the *play*, in which one of the players tries to fulfill the contract.

The auction is a conversation among the players, using the language of bridge. It's started by the player who dealt the cards and continues, in clockwise fashion, around the table. At this point, you won't be familiar with the language of bridge, but you can listen to the sound of the auction.

North starts with, "One Club."

East says, "One Heart."

South, the player whose hand we're looking at, says, "One Spade."

"Pass," says West.

"Two Spades," from North.

"Pass," by East.

South says—or bids—"Four Spades."

"Pass," from West.

"Pass," from North, South's partner.

"Pass," by East.

The auction has come to an end. Everyone has had a say, and a contract has been agreed upon. There are many things to explain about bridge, and I'll have to ask you to be patient. Each delightful segment of the game will be unwrapped, in time. For now, I'll tell you that the North-South partnership has won the auction and settled on a contract of "Four Spades." In a bridge book or a newspaper column, the conversation would be recorded in this manner:

WEST	NORTH	EAST	SOUTH
	1♣	1♥	1♠
Pass	2♠	Pass	4♠
Pass	Pass	Pass	

More about the bidding later. For now, let's see what happens next. The auction is over, and it's time for the play. West selects a card and places it face up on the table. It's the ten of hearts (♥10). This is the *opening lead*.

Now North's cards are all placed face up on the table, with each suit arranged in a vertical column facing toward South.

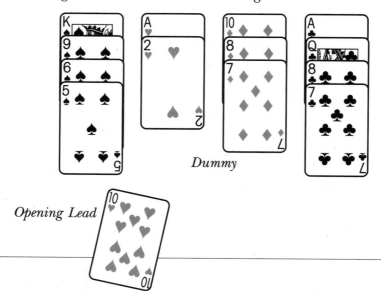

Dummy

Opening Lead

"Thank you, partner," says South

You might wonder why West placed only one card face up on the table, and North then faced all thirteen cards on the table. How does North feel as the only player whose entire hand is exposed? Actually, North is on the sidelines, so to speak. North-South won the auction, and South will be trying to fulfill, or *make*, the contract by playing the cards from both the North and the South hands. In the language of the game, South is referred to as the *declarer*, and North's hand is referred to as the *dummy*. South is "up to bat" for the partnership. We'll see later on how the auction determines which player is the declarer and which player is the dummy.

East and West are referred to as the *defenders*. They'll be trying to stop South from fulfilling the contract during the play. The player to the left of declarer, West in this case, makes the opening lead before the dummy is placed on the table. From that point on, everyone can see dummy's cards during the play of the hand.

In newspaper columns and bridge books, the North and South players' hands and the opening lead might be shown in this fashion:

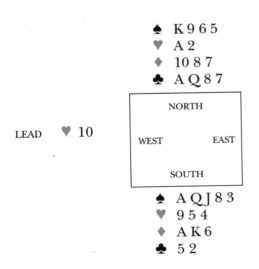

Sometimes, all four hands are shown; sometimes, only declarer's and dummy's hands. Throughout this book, dummy's hand will appear in a shaded box so that you can see which cards are placed face up on the table. Where appropriate, the opening lead will also

be shaded. The complete deal we're watching might be represented
in this manner.

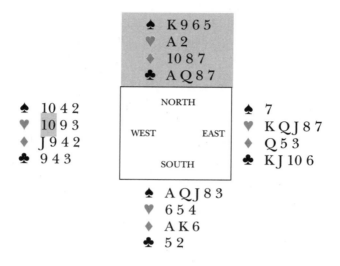

South asks North to play the ♥A from the dummy because South
is now directing the play for the partnership. East plays the ♥8 face
up on the table, and South places the ♥4 on the table.

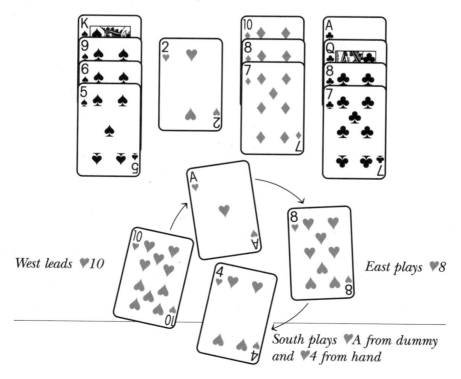

West leads ♥10   East plays ♥8

South plays ♥A from dummy
and ♥4 from hand

Once everyone has seen all four cards, South gathers them up and places them face down on the table in a small pile. This is the first round of play. The four cards, one contributed in turn from each hand, constitute a *trick*, and as will become clearer in the next chapter, North-South have won the first trick.

The play continues in a similar fashion until the players have no cards left. By this time, thirteen rounds, or tricks, have been played. There are ten small piles in front of South, indicating that North-South won ten of the tricks, and the remaining three tricks belong to the East-West partnership.

"Well done, partner," comments North. "You made the contract."

"Yes, you played it nicely," East remarks.

"Thank you," says South. "I'll enter it on the scoresheet."

"Thank you for letting us watch your game," we say. "We'd like to stay longer, but we're meeting friends for tea." A cup of tea with some scones and jam would be enjoyable indeed!

Summary

Bridge is a card game played with four people who sit opposite one another in partnerships. The game starts with one player dealing the cards face down in clockwise rotation until each player has thirteen cards. The players pick up their hands and sort the cards into suits with the high cards in each suit on the left.

The deal starts off with an auction. Each player gets a chance to bid and compete for the contract. Once the contract has been decided, one member of the side which won the contract becomes the declarer and will play both hands for the partnership. The other partnership becomes the defenders. The defender to the left of declarer makes an opening lead by placing a card face up on the table, and declarer's partner then places the entire hand face up on the table, as the dummy.

The deal is then played out in thirteen rounds, or tricks. A card is played from each of the four hands to make up a trick. Declarer is trying to take enough tricks to make the contract. The defenders are trying to stop declarer from fulfilling the contract.

Exercises

1. What number would best describe each of the following:

a) The cards from the deck used in a bridge game. *52*

b) The suits in a deck. *4*

c) The cards in each suit. *13*

d) The honor cards in a suit. *5*

e) The high cards in a suit. *4*

f) The players in a bridge game. *4*

g) The players in a partnership. *2*

h) The cards in a player's hand at the beginning of the game. *13*

i) The cards played to a trick. *4*

j) The tricks available in a bridge hand. *13*

Answers to Exercises

a) All **52** cards are used in a bridge game.

b) There are **4** suits: clubs, diamonds, hearts, and spades.

c) There are **13** cards in each suit.

d) There are **5** honor cards in each suit: ace, king, queen, jack, and ten.

e) There are **4** high cards in each suit: ace, king, queen, jack.

f) There are **4** players in a bridge game.

g) There are **2** players in each partnership.

h) There are **13** cards in a bridge hand.

i) There are **4** cards played to each trick.

j) There are **13** tricks available in a bridge hand.

Taking Tricks

"Bridge is not a standardized test to measure your intelligence or the intelligence of your friends— it's a game."

When I'm asked to explain bridge in ten words or fewer, I say that it's a trick-taking game. Before going any further, you need to know what a trick is and how tricks are won and lost.

Tricks are often won with the high cards in each suit. The lower cards also have their role to play. An important part of the game is learning how to make the best use of your high cards, and how to develop the lower-ranking cards so that they that can also win tricks.

The Trick

A trick is started when one player leads a card, placing it face up on the table. The other players, in clockwise rotation, then play a card from the same suit that was led. Let's take a look at the first trick that was played in the game we were watching:

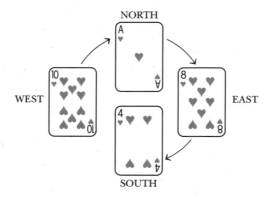

West led the ♥10, the ♥A was played from the North hand, East contributed the ♥8 and then South played the ♥4. That completed the first trick. Since a heart was led originally, each of the players also played a card from the heart suit on the trick. This is referred to as *following suit* and is an important rule of the game. You must play a card in the same suit that was originally led, if you have one. You'll see a little later what you do when you can't "follow suit."

In the game we were watching, North's hand was put down as the dummy after the "opening lead" of the ♥10, and South, as declarer, actually selected the card to be played from North's hand. The basic concept of a trick still applied. A card in the same suit was played from each hand in turn, in a clockwise direction.

Since the cards are ranked within each suit, North's ♥A was the highest card played in the suit that was led, and the North hand wins the trick. Unless there's a trump suit—which will be introduced in a moment—the highest card played in the suit that was led wins the trick. Since North and South are partners, the trick is won by the North-South partnership.

The next important rule is that the player winning a trick leads to the next trick. In the above example, North won the first trick, and so the lead to the next trick comes from the North hand. Any suit can be led at this point; you don't have to continue leading the suit in which you won the trick. For example, a spade could now be led from the North hand, and the second trick might look like this:

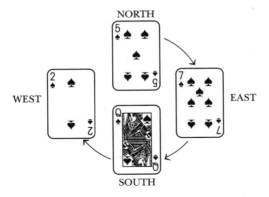

South's ♠Q wins the second trick because it's the highest card played to the trick. You might wonder why South didn't play the ♠A on this trick, the highest card in the suit. Although you have to follow suit, you don't have to play your highest card to a trick, and you don't have to win the trick even if you can. North and South hold the ♠A, ♠K and ♠Q between them, so it's necessary only to play the queen to win the trick.

South won the second trick and will now choose a card to lead to the third trick. South could lead another spade or choose a card from a different suit. The play continues in this manner until all thirteen tricks have been played out.

The Opening Lead

In the hand we were watching, West led to the first trick. To get the play started, the opening lead is always made by the player to the left of declarer. South was the declarer of the contract, West made the opening lead, and North put down the hand as dummy. South won't always be the declarer—the declarer is decided based on the auction—but the same principle always applies. If West were declaring the contract, North, the player on West's left, would make the opening lead, and East, West's partner, would put down the dummy. Then, the play would follow the same flow, with the player winning the first trick leading to the second trick, and so on.

Discarding

If you have no cards left in the suit that's led, you play a card from another suit. This is called *discarding*. For example:

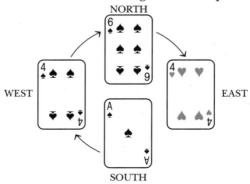

South leads the ♠A, West follows suit with the ♠4, North plays the ♠6, and East, with no spades left, discards the ♥4. You choose a card to discard that you don't think you'll need later on in the play of the hand.

Keeping Track

There are two ways to keep track of the tricks that have been won and lost by each side. In most forms of the game, as each trick is won, the four cards played to the trick are gathered up by one member of the partnership winning the trick. The cards are stacked into a neat pile, and placed face down near the edge of the table. Only one member of each partnership collects the tricks, making it easier to see how many tricks have been won or lost. As each trick is gathered in, it's offset slightly from the previous tricks so that it's easy to count up the number of tricks at the end of the hand. At the end of play, the table might look like this:

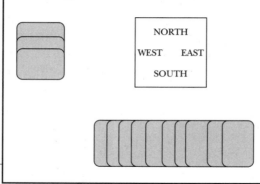

The North-South partnership has won ten of the thirteen tricks. The East-West partnership has won the other three.

In tournament bridge, a different method is used to keep track of the tricks won and lost. After determining which side won the trick, each player turns the card face down, pointing in the direction of the partnership that won the trick. At the end of play, the table might look like this:

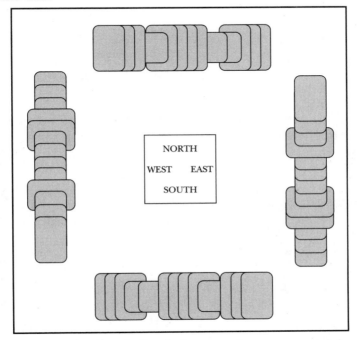

In this example, North-South have again won ten tricks—those pointing in their direction—and East-West have won three.

The Trump Suit

A bridge hand can be played in notrump or in a trump suit. This is determined during the auction. If a contract is declared in *notrump*, the highest card played in the suit led always wins the trick. If a contract is played with a *trump suit*, one of the suits takes on special significance. When a card from the trump suit is played to a trick, it wins the trick unless a higher card from the trump suit is played to the same trick.

For example, suppose spades have been named as the trump suit during the auction. A trick might look like this:

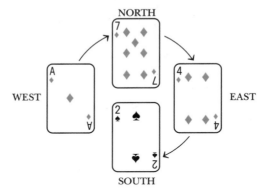

West leads the ♦A, North plays the ♦7, East plays the ♦4, and South plays the ♠2. Because of the power of the trump suit, South wins the trick even though the ♠2 is much lower-ranking than the ♦A. South is said to be *trumping* or *ruffing* the trick.

The earlier rules about tricks still apply. South can play a trump card on this trick only if South has no more diamonds. South doesn't have to play a trump on this trick. South could discard a heart or a club, allowing West to win the trick with the ♦A.

You can lead the trump suit at any point during the play when it's your turn to lead to the next trick. If the trump suit is led, the players must follow suit if they can. For example:

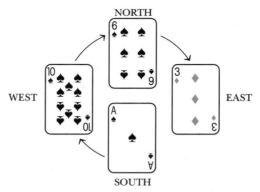

South leads the ♠A, West follows suit with the ♠10, North contributes the ♠6, and East, with no spades left, discards the ♦3. South wins the trick, having played the highest trump card to the trick.

Developing Tricks

If there's no trump suit, an ace will always win the trick if it's led—no one will have a higher card. There are only four aces, so many of the tricks will be won with lower-ranking cards. Once an ace has been played to a trick, the king becomes the highest remaining card in the suit and—again assuming there's no trump suit—can be used to win the next trick in the suit. Now the queen becomes the highest-ranking card in the suit.

It might seem as though the first four tricks could be taken with the aces, the next four with the kings, then the queens, and so forth. The play of the hand, however, is usually far more interesting. Both partnerships are trying to win tricks at the same time, so high cards often fall on the same trick.

Bridge is a partnership game. The cards in the partnership hands can work together. Let's take a quick look at the basic methods used to help win tricks for the partnership.

In each of the following examples, we'll be considering only the cards in a single suit held by the four players, not the complete hand. The symbols for the cards are used to represent the cards themselves in each diagram. You might want to take the heart suit from your deck of cards and lay out each example as it's discussed.

Promotion

The most straightforward method of creating a winner is through the technique of *promotion*. By using your side's high cards to drive out the higher cards in the other hands, you can promote lower-ranking cards into winners. Consider this layout of the heart suit in the four hands.

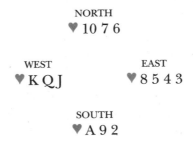

NORTH
♥ 10 7 6

WEST   EAST
♥ K Q J   ♥ 8 5 4 3

SOUTH
♥ A 9 2

North-South have the highest card in the heart suit, the ace, which will win a trick. West, however, can establish future winners in the heart suit by leading one of the hearts, the ♥K for example. This will drive out South's ♥A, if the North-South partnership wants to win the trick. The remaining cards in the heart suit now look like this:

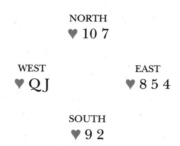

NORTH
♥ 10 7

WEST
♥ Q J

EAST
♥ 8 5 4

SOUTH
♥ 9 2

West's ♥Q and ♥J have been promoted into the two highest-ranking cards in the suit, and East-West will be able to win tricks with these cards when they next have the opportunity to lead to a trick.

Notice that East-West have to let North-South win a trick in order to promote their own winning tricks. This is a common theme in developing tricks. You often have to let the other side win a trick in order to establish future winning tricks for your side. The partnership shouldn't expect to be able to win all its tricks right away. There's a little work to be done. A partnership can work nicely together to get tricks from a suit like this:

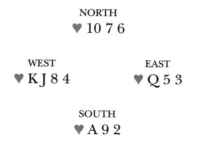

NORTH
♥ 10 7 6

WEST
♥ K J 8 4

EAST
♥ Q 5 3

SOUTH
♥ A 9 2

West can't do all the work alone, but the East-West partnership can still promote winning tricks in the heart suit with a little cooperation. For example, West could lead the ♥4 and, if the ♥6 is played from the North hand, East could play the ♥Q to drive out South's ace. West's ♥K is now promoted into the highest card in the suit, and the ♥J has been promoted into the second highest card in the suit.

Long Suits

Do you think you could win a trick with a two? Consider this layout of the heart suit:

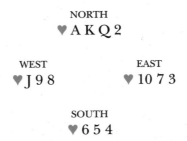

NORTH
♥ A K Q 2

WEST   EAST
♥ J 9 8   ♥ 10 7 3

SOUTH
♥ 6 5 4

North-South have only the top three cards in the heart suit, but they can take four tricks by leading the suit. After winning the first three tricks with the ♥A, ♥K, and ♥Q, the suit now looks like this:

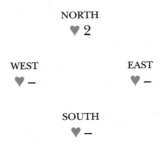

NORTH
♥ 2

WEST   EAST
♥ –   ♥ –

SOUTH
♥ –

North is the only player with a heart left because the other players had to follow suit each time hearts were led. North can now lead the ♥2, the lowest-ranking card in the suit, and this low card will win the trick—assuming the contract is being played without a trump suit or that hearts are trump. All the other players will have to discard from other suits. The technique used is to continue to lead the suit until the other side has no cards left. This is referred to as establishment through length.

Establishing tricks through length won't always work. It depends on how the missing cards are divided in the other hands. Suppose we make a slight change to the layout of the heart suit:

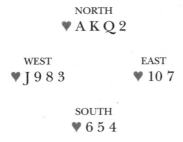

If North now takes tricks with the ♥A, ♥K, and ♥Q, the remaining cards look like this:

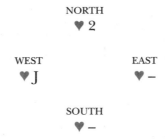

Now it's West, not North, who will win the trick if hearts are led again. This is why low cards win tricks only some of the time. Learning how to take tricks with your low cards is one of the many interesting facets of the game.

The Finesse

A *finesse* is an attempt to take a trick with a card when the other side has a higher-ranking card. Suppose you're the South player, and this is the layout of the heart suit:

NORTH
♥ 3 2

WEST   EAST
♥ 10 9 7 6   ♥ A Q J 8 5

SOUTH
♥ K 4

If you need to win a trick in the heart suit, it's unlikely to do much good if you lead the king. East has a higher-ranking card, the ace, and you have no lower-ranking cards to promote. If you lead the ♥K, East-West can win all the tricks in the heart suit. It's possible, however, to give yourself a chance of winning a trick with your king by carefully arranging the order in which the cards are played to the trick.

Instead of leading the king, start the trick by leading a low heart from the North hand. East must now play a card before you have to play your card to the trick. If East plays the ♥A, you can play the ♥4, and your ♥K will be the winner the next time the suit is played. If East chooses not to play the ace, you can play the king and win the trick, since West has no higher card to play. This is the essence of the finesse. You lead toward the card you hope will win a trick. The order that you play the cards is important.

This won't always work. Suppose this is the layout of the heart suit:

NORTH
♥ 3 2

WEST   EAST
♥ A Q J 8 5   ♥ 10 9 7 6

SOUTH
♥ K 4

Leading a heart from the North hand toward South's king will be of no benefit when West holds the ♥A. South will have to play a card to the trick before West. If South plays the king, West will win the trick with the ace. If South doesn't play the king, West can win with a lower card. The success of a finesse will depend on the location of the missing high cards—another interesting facet of the game.

Using the Trump Suit

A trump suit can have a dramatic effect on the number of tricks that either side can win. Suppose this is the layout of the heart suit in the four hands:

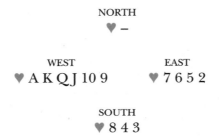

```
                     NORTH
                      ♥ —

       WEST                    EAST
   ♥ A K Q J 10 9           ♥ 7 6 5 2

                     SOUTH
                    ♥ 8 4 3
```

If there's no trump suit, and West starts leading hearts, there's nothing North-South can do to prevent West from taking six tricks in the suit. If one of the other suits, spades for example, has been made the trump suit during the auction, things take on a different perspective. North-South may be able to prevent East-West from taking even one heart trick! Every time hearts are led, North may be able to win the trick by trumping, or ruffing, with a low spade.

Naturally, during the auction, East-West will try to get the contract played with hearts as the trump suit, but as you'll see in upcoming chapters, there's no guarantee that East-West will win the auction and get to choose the trump suit.

Decisions, Decisions

In the actual play of the hand, you don't see the layout of each suit in all four hands. The declarer has a slight advantage because the dummy is placed face up on the table. Declarer can see the strength and weakness in each of the combined suits.

The defenders have a more difficult task. When choosing the opening lead, the defender on declarer's left can see none of the other three hands. Even after the opening lead is made, and the dummy is put down on the table, the defenders can't see the cards held by each other. This provides the challenge of figuring out the best way to play each suit when you can't see your partner's cards.

Throughout the play of the hand, both the declarer and the defenders are faced with decisions about which card to play to each trick. The order in which the cards are played can have a large impact on the outcome of the hand—how many tricks are won or lost by each side.

Here are some general guidelines which should prove useful when you're wondering which card to play. It can make a difference whether you're contributing the first card to the trick—*first hand*— the second card to the trick—*second hand*—the third card—*third hand*—or the final card—*fourth hand*. Each position has advantages and disadvantages.

First Hand

Playing first to a trick is a big advantage. You choose the suit to be played and the card you want to lead in the suit. You want to pick the suit that is most likely to provide your side with the maximum number of tricks. That doesn't mean that you should always be trying to take tricks right away with your high cards. Sometimes, you have to let the other side win tricks in order to establish future winning tricks for your side. It's tempting to play your high cards first. It's like a race: the runner with the best start doesn't necessarily win.

For example, suppose there's no trump suit, and you have to make the opening lead from this hand:

♠ 7 2
♥ A 10 6
♦ 10 8 6 5
♣ K Q J 10

You could lead the ♥A and be certain of winning the first trick for your side. The drawback is that leading the ace is unlikely to gain any further tricks for your side. Partner might have the ♥K, and your side can take a second trick in the suit. It's more likely that you helped the opponents. For example, the layout of the heart suit might be something like this:

NORTH
♥ Q 8 2

WEST (FIRST HAND)   EAST
♥ A 10 6   ♥ J 7 5 3

SOUTH
♥ K 9 4

If West leads the ♥A, North-South will get the next two tricks in the suit: one with ♥K, and one with the ♥Q.

Look at the hand again. A better choice would be to lead a club. You might not win the first trick—if the opposing partnership holds the ♣A—but once that card has been driven out, you'll have promoted your remaining three club cards as potential winning tricks. Better yet, you still have the ♥A.

Once the opening lead has been made, the dummy is placed face up on the table. Now that everyone can see at least half the cards, it becomes a little easier for each side to see opportunities to develop or win tricks. Declarer has the advantage of being able to see both hands of the partnership, and can use this knowledge to apply the techniques of promotion, suit establishment through length, and the finesse. This helps declarer decide what to lead after winning a trick.

The defenders have their own resources. They make the opening lead, giving them the first opportunity to take or establish tricks. They can give each other information through the cards they choose to play during the hand. More on that later.

Second Hand

Suppose the first time the heart suit is played the player on your right leads the ♥4, and you have to choose which card to play when you've the ♥A, ♥10, and ♥6. You're in the position of playing the second card to a trick. You can often follow the guideline of playing second hand low. That suggests that you would play your ♥6.

The reason behind this guideline is that your partner will be playing the last card to the trick. There's no hurry for you to make a commitment in second position. For example, this might be the layout of the heart suit when declarer leads the ♥4 toward the dummy:

NORTH
♥ Q 8 2

WEST (SECOND HAND)   EAST
♥ A 10 6   ♥ J 7 5 3

SOUTH (FIRST HAND)
♥ K 9 4

If South leads the ♥4, and West plays the ♥A right away, the remaining cards will look like this after the trick is over:

NORTH
♥ Q 8

WEST   EAST
♥ 10 6   ♥ J 7 5

SOUTH
♥ K 9

West will have won the first trick in the heart suit, but North-South will later get two tricks: one with the ♥K, and one with the ♥Q.

Go back to the first layout of the suit. If West uses instead the guideline of second hand low and plays the ♥6 on the first trick, North will have to play the ♥Q to prevent East from winning the trick. The remaining cards now look like this:

NORTH
♥ 8 2

WEST   EAST
♥ A 10   ♥ J 7 5

SOUTH
♥ K 9

North-South have won one trick in the suit but will have difficulty taking any more tricks. If a heart is later led from dummy, whether South plays the ♥K or ♥9, West will be able to win the trick by playing one of the carefully preserved higher hearts. North-South get only one trick in the suit, rather than two.

Second hand low is only a guideline, not a rule. It will help you do something when you aren't sure which is the best card to play. As you become more familiar with how tricks are won or lost, you'll find it easier to decide which card will work best in various situations.

Third Hand

Let's suppose the first time the heart suit is played your partner leads the ♥3, the next hand plays the ♥2, and you have to choose which card to play when you hold the ♥Q, ♥9, and ♥4. You're the third player contributing a card to the trick. When you aren't sure what to do, there's a guideline in this position also: third hand high. You would play your ♥Q. This is the last chance for your side.

Your ♥Q might not win the trick but it could do some good for your side anyway. This might be the complete layout of the heart suit:

NORTH (SECOND HAND)
♥ 8 7 2

WEST (FIRST HAND) EAST (THIRD HAND)
♥ K J 6 3 ♥ Q 9 4

SOUTH
♥ A 10 5

West leads the ♥3, and the ♥2 is played from the North hand. It's East's turn to play. If East plays the ♥4, South will win the trick with the ♥5. Even if East plays the ♥9, South will win the trick with the ♥10 and still have the ♥A left to win a second trick in the suit. East should play the ♥Q, third hand high. Now South must play the ♥A to win the trick.

Although East-West haven't won the first trick, the remaining cards in the suit look like this:

NORTH
♥ 8 7

WEST   EAST
♥ K J 6   ♥ 9 4

SOUTH
♥ 10 5

West's ♥K and ♥J have been promoted into the highest cards in the heart suit, and East-West are poised to win some tricks in the suit when they next have the opportunity to lead.

There are many situations that can come up when you're in a position to play the third card to a trick. For example, the card that was led from partner's hand might already be high enough to win the trick, so there's no need for you to play your highest card. The guideline, however, will serve you in those situations where the best choice is not clear.

Fourth Hand

Playing last to a trick is a big advantage. You can see the cards played by the other three hands. Your side may have already won the trick, in which case you don't have to use one of your high cards. You may not have a card high enough to win the trick, in which case you can play a low card, keeping your bigger cards for later. Otherwise, you have the opportunity to win the trick for your side, playing only as high a card as is necessary to win the trick.

Summary

Bridge is a trick-taking game. When the auction is over, the hand is played out, one trick at a time. Each trick consists of four cards, one contributed by each player. Here are the rules for playing to each trick:

- The opening lead is made by the player to the left of declarer by placing any card face up on the table. After this, the dummy is put down.
- A card is played face up, in clockwise rotation, from each of the other three hands to complete the trick.
- Players must play a card from the same suit that was originally led, when possible.
- If a player has no cards left in the suit led, a card from another suit may be played.
- In a notrump contract, the highest-ranking card played in the suit that was led always wins the trick.
- If there's a trump suit, a card played from the trump suit automatically wins the trick unless a higher trump card is played to the same trick.
- The hand which wins the trick leads to the next trick.

There are a number of techniques that can be used when a partnership is trying to win tricks:

- Promotion.
- Establishing tricks from long suits.
- The finesse.
- Trumping.

continued next page

Use the following guidelines when playing to a trick:

- First hand—Lead the suit most likely to provide your side with the maximum number of tricks.
- Second hand—Play a low card unless there's clearly a better choice.
- Third hand—Try to win the trick for your side by playing as high a card as necessary.
- Fourth hand—Decide which card to play only after seeing all the other cards played to the trick.

Exercises

1. In each of the tricks shown below, hearts are the trump suit and the card led to each trick is highlighted. Which partnership wins the trick? Which player would lead to the next trick?

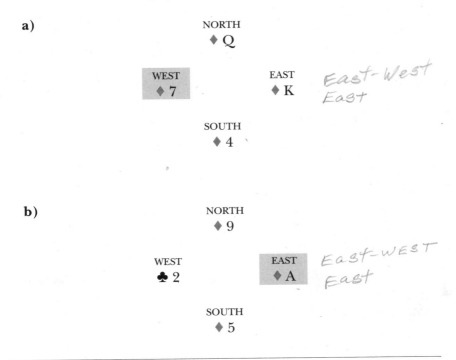

a)

NORTH
♦ Q

WEST
♦ 7

EAST
♦ K   *East-West*
        East

SOUTH
♦ 4

b)

NORTH
♦ 9

WEST
♣ 2

EAST
♦ A   *East-WEST*
        East

SOUTH
♦ 5

c)

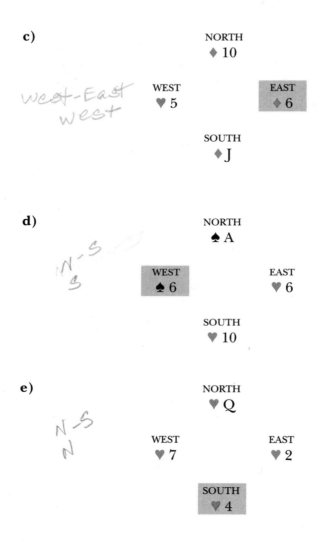

NORTH
♦ 10

West–East
West

WEST
♥ 5

EAST
♦ 6

SOUTH
♦ J

d)

N–S
3

NORTH
♠ A

WEST
♠ 6

EAST
♥ 6

SOUTH
♥ 10

e)

N–S
N

NORTH
♥ Q

WEST
♥ 7

EAST
♥ 2

SOUTH
♥ 4

2. *(Facing page)*With no trump suit, how many tricks are North-South likely to be able to take in the diamond suit in each of the following layouts? How would they go about taking their tricks?

a)

NORTH
♦ A K 4

WEST   *4*   EAST
♦ 9 6   ♦ 10 8 5 3

SOUTH
♦ Q J 7 2

b)

NORTH
♦ 8 7 3

WEST   *3*   EAST
♦ A 9 5 2   ♦ 6 4

SOUTH
♦ K Q J 10

c)

NORTH
♦ A K Q 3 2

WEST   *5*   EAST
♦ 10 8   ♦ J 7 6

SOUTH
♦ 9 5 4

d)

NORTH
♦ 8 6 4

WEST   *1*   EAST
♦ J 9 7   ♦ A Q 10 3

SOUTH
♦ K 5 2

Answers to Exercises

1a) **East-West**. East's ♦K wins the trick because it's the highest card played in the suit led. East leads to the next trick.

1b) **East-West**. East's ♦A wins the trick. West discarded a club. East leads to the next trick.

1c) **East-West**. Although South played the highest diamond on the trick, West wins the trick by playing a trump card. West leads to the next trick.

1d) **North-South**. Both East and South played a trump on this trick. South wins by playing the higher trump. South leads to the next trick.

1e) **North-South**. When everyone plays a trump to the trick, the highest trump wins. North's ♥Q wins the trick, and North will lead to the next trick.

2a) **Four**. North could win the first two tricks with the ♦A and ♦K and then lead the ♦4. South would win the next two tricks with the ♦Q and ♦J.

2b) **Three**. South could lead a diamond and West would have to play the ♦A to win the trick. South will now have promoted three potential diamond winners in the suit.

2c) **Five**. After winning the first three tricks with the ♦A-K-Q, North will be the only player with any diamonds left. North can take two more tricks with the ♦3 and ♦2, which have become winners due to the length of the suit in North's hand.

2d) **One**. To get a trick from the diamond suit, North-South will need to arrange to lead a diamond from the North hand. East must decide whether or not to win the trick with the ace before South has to choose a card. Sooner or later, South will get a trick with the ♦K. This is the technique of a finesse.

The Auction

"What is the use of a book," thought Alice, "without pictures or conversations?"

— LEWIS CARROLL,
Alice's Adventures in Wonderland
[1865]

Let's go back to the bridge game we were watching at Brown's Hotel and listen to the conversation. The players picked up their hands and sorted the cards into suits. Then they started talking in an unfamiliar language. North said, "One Club," and East said "One Heart." This was the beginning of the auction, and the players were using the language of bidding.

The auction is a discussion among the four people at the table. It's like any conversation. Sometimes one person is talking, and everyone else is listening. Two people may be exchanging information while the other two people are listening. Everyone could have something to say.

The objective of the auction is to come to an agreement on the contract. The contract is a commitment to take a certain number of tricks during the play of the hand, either with a trump suit or in notrump. The partnership willing to contract for the most number of tricks wins the auction and gets to play the hand with their choice of trump suit, or notrump.

If you were to go to a regular auction, you'd be bidding on your own. Bridge is a little different. You're bidding along with your partner, and the two of you must come to a consensus on the best contract for the partnership. At the same time, the other partnership is competing for the right to buy the contract and name the trump suit.

In an auction, the price gets higher with each round of bidding until no one wants to bid any higher. A bidding conversation in bridge works the same way. The bidding continues to escalate until one side or the other can't afford to bid any more. Sometimes, one side doesn't even bother to compete for the contract. At other times, the bridge auction is very competitive, and the bids get higher and higher. We'll see how this works as we go along.

The Language of Bidding

The bridge conversation uses its own special language. It's not very difficult to learn because there are only seven numbers and eight words making up the entire vocabulary. The numbers go from one to seven. The eight words: clubs, diamonds, hearts, spades, notrump, pass, double, and redouble.

Making a Bid

Other than pass, double, and redouble, a *bid* consists of a number followed by the name of a suit or notrump.

First of all, there's the number. This is frequently referred to as the _level_. It represents the number of tricks that you're committing to take. It may sound as if a bid at the one level—"One Heart," for example—is a commitment to take only one trick, but in fact, it's a commitment to take seven tricks—one more than the average number available during the play.

There are thirteen tricks to be won each time a hand is played. The average number of tricks you would expect each partnership to win would be six and a half. It would be inconvenient to tear tricks in half—expensive too! To win the auction, you would expect to commit to taking more than half the tricks, so the lowest number of tricks you can contract to take is seven. The first six tricks are referred to as "the book," and the number you call when making a bid is added to the book when determining how many tricks must be won to fulfill the contract. Any bid at the one level requires 1 + 6 = 7 tricks.

A bid of "Four Spades," therefore, is a commitment to take 4 + 6 = 10 tricks. This is why the numbers in the bidding language go up to only seven. A bid at the seven level, such as "Seven Diamonds," would be a contract to take all thirteen tricks (7 + 6 = 13).

As you've probably guessed by now, the second part of the bid is the suggested *denomination*—a trump suit or notrump. A bid of "One Heart" is a commitment to take seven tricks with hearts as the trump suit. A bid of "Six Notrump" is a commitment to take twelve (6 + 6) tricks with no trump suit.

When writing down the bidding, numbers and symbols are usually used in place of the words. A bid of "One Heart" would be written as 1♥. A bid of "Three Notrump" is recorded as 3NT.

Starting the Auction

The auction starts with the player who dealt out the cards. The dealer makes a *call*, either bidding or passing. The auction proceeds clockwise around the table so that every player gets a chance to say something. Each player can pass or make a bid. The first person to make a bid is called the *opening bidder*. The opening bid doesn't have to start at the one level, but it usually does.

The Bidding Levels

Suppose the opening bidder says 1♣, contracting to take seven tricks with clubs as the trump suit. The next player says 1♥, contracting to take seven tricks with hearts as the trump suit. The player after that says 1♠, also contracting for seven tricks, but with spades as the trump suit. Which is the highest bid for the contract?

To resolve this, the suits are ranked in alphabetical order, starting with clubs as the lowest, then diamonds, hearts, and spades. Notrump is ranked at the top of the list. A bid of 1♠, therefore, ranks higher than a bid of 1♥. A bid of 1♦ ranks higher than 1♣.

The only rule is that the auction is like a one-way street. You must keep moving in one direction. To stay on the same level, you must bid a higher-ranking suit, or notrump. If you want to bid a suit that's lower ranking than the last bid, you have to move up a level. If the auction is already at 1♠, for example, and you want to make diamonds the trump suit, you would have to bid 2♦ rather than 1♦. This is how the bidding escalates during the auction.

There are seven levels with the suits ranked within each level:

7♣	7♦	7♥	7♠	7NT	*Highest Bid*
6♣	6♦	6♥	6♠	6NT	
5♣	5♦	5♥	5♠	5NT	
4♣	4♦	4♥	4♠	4NT	
3♣	3♦	3♥	3♠	3NT	
2♣	2♦	2♥	2♠	2NT	
Lowest Bid 1♣	1♦	1♥	1♠	1NT	

The lowest is the one level, which represents seven tricks—one more than "the book," or average. The highest is the seven level. That makes sense because a bid at the seven level is a contract to take all of the thirteen available tricks.

The auction can start at any level, with an opening bid of 3♣, for example. You can jump levels if you wish, but you can't go back. After a bid of 1♥, a bid of 2♦ would be sufficient, but you could jump to 3♦ or higher. We'll see later on how the players make the best use of the bidding structure.

Ending the Auction

At an auction, the bidding usually finishes with, "Going once...going twice...sold." A bridge auction ends when a bid is followed by three passes. Essentially, everyone is agreeing that the last bid made will be the contract.

Let's bring back that first auction we heard:

WEST	NORTH (DEALER)	EAST	SOUTH
	1♣	1♥	1♠
Pass	2♠	Pass	4♠
Pass	Pass	Pass	

The three passes following the 4♠ bid completed the auction. The contract of 4♠ was accepted by all the players. No one wanted to bid higher.

Everyone does get a chance to bid on the first round of the auction. If the first three players say pass, the fourth player can open the bidding. It's only after the bidding has started that three successive passes end the auction.

Are you wondering why North-South bid up to 4♠, committing to take ten tricks, when they might have stopped at 1♠? It's time to look at the scoring.

Scoring

The auction determines the contract, and the hand is then played out to see whether the contract can be fulfilled, or *made*, by the side winning the auction. At the end of play, the result is entered on a score pad. Points are won for bidding and making a contract. Points can also be won by *defeating* a contract played by the other partnership. For now, we'll cover the essentials. If you want more details, turn to the section on scoring in the appendix.

Trick Score

For making a contract, you receive a *trick score* for the number of tricks you bid. The trick score depends on the denomination of the contract as follows:

♣ or ♦ (minor suits)	20 points per trick
♥ or ♠ (major suits)	30 points per trick
Notrump	40 points for the first trick plus
	30 points per trick thereafter

A contract of two hearts (2♥) would have a trick score of 60 points (30 + 30) if it's made. You have to take eight tricks to make a contract of 2♥, but you don't get any trick score for the first six tricks—your book. A contract of two notrump (2NT) would be worth 70 points (40 + 30).

Bonuses

In addition to the trick score, there are bonuses for reaching certain levels. If a contract has a trick score of 100 or more points, you receive a *game bonus*. Since the trick score is different depending on the denomination, the contracts you aim for in order to receive the game bonus are:

3NT	40 + 30 + 30 = 100
4♥ or 4♠	30 + 30 + 30 + 30 = 120
5♣ or 5♦	20 + 20 + 20 + 20 + 20 = 100

The game contracts are highlighted in the bidding levels. 3NT requires only nine tricks, so it's a popular contract. 4♥ and 4♠ require ten tricks, so they're the most popular game contracts when you do want to play with a trump suit. 5♣ and 5♦ require eleven tricks to succeed, so they're avoided. Much of the strategy in the bidding centers around trying to reach the best contract.

The auction will often stop short of the game level when neither partnership feels it has enough combined strength to commit to a game level contract. Any contract worth fewer than 100 points is called a *partscore*. A contract of 4♦, for example, is worth only 80 points (20 + 20 + 20 + 20) and is a partscore contract even though you'll have to take ten tricks to make it.

In addition to the game bonus, the partnership can receive a *small slam* bonus for bidding and making a contract at the six level—taking twelve of the thirteen tricks. There's an even larger bonus for bidding and making a *grand slam*—a contract to take all thirteen tricks.

Overtricks and Undertricks

You receive the additional trick score for making more tricks than required to fulfill the contract. If you take ten tricks in a contract of 2♠, for example, you receive your trick score of 60 points for making the contract plus 30 points for each of the extra tricks, or *overtricks*, for a total of 120 points. You don't get the game bonus, however. You would have to have reached a contract of 4♠ to get the game bonus for bidding and making the contract.

If you don't take the number of tricks required to make your contract, the other partnership collects points. These are referred to as *penalty* points. Suppose you bid 3NT and contracted to take nine tricks. As it turns out, you take only seven tricks. The other partnership would receive a bonus for the two *undertricks* by which they defeated the contract.

Doubles and Redoubles

Two of the words in the bidding language which don't appear on the bidding levels are "double" and "redouble." These are bids which can be used during the auction to increase the score if the contract is made or defeated.

If you don't think the other side can make their contract, you can double when it's your turn to bid. If the double is followed by three passes, the auction is over, and the contract is doubled. This will increase the score if the contract is made and also increase the penalty for undertricks if the contract is defeated.

If your contract has been doubled, you can redouble when it's your turn to bid, and if this is followed by three passes, the contract is played redoubled. As you can imagine, this further increases the score for making or defeating the contract.

The scoring for doubled and redoubled contracts is included in the appendix. Special meanings are sometimes associated with doubles and redoubles during the auction, and we'll be looking at one such case in the chapter on competitive bidding. For now, you need to know only that such bids exist.

Decisions Made During the Bidding

The bidding comes before the play of the hand because the information that comes out of the auction is needed before the play can start. The bidding determines four things: the contract, the declarer, the dummy, and the player who makes the opening lead.

Now that you know a little more about how the bidding works, let's go back and listen to the auction we overheard while watching the game at Brown's Hotel.

WEST	NORTH	EAST	SOUTH
	1♣	1♥	1♠
Pass	2♠	Pass	4♠
Pass	Pass	Pass	

North was the dealer and had the first opportunity to bid or pass. North decided to *open the bidding* with a bid of 1♣. The bidding moved clockwise around the table, and East had the next chance to speak and bid 1♥. East didn't have to move up a level because hearts are higher ranking than clubs. South bid 1♠. South didn't have to move to a higher level because spades rank higher than hearts. West decided to pass. North now bid 2♠. As we'll see later, this told South that North agreed that spades would make a good trump suit for the partnership. East didn't want to bid any more and passed.

Although the auction might have ended here, South decided that the partnership should go for the game bonus and jumped all the way to 4♠. This bid was followed by three passes, ending the auction. Let's see what has been decided.

The Contract

The last bid, 4♠, becomes the contract. North-South have to take ten tricks (4 + 6) with spades as the trump suit. If they make the contract, they'll receive a trick score of 120 points (30 + 30 + 30 + 30). They'll also get a game bonus, since the contract is worth 100 or more points. If they don't make ten tricks, East-West will receive a score for defeating the contract.

Declarer and Dummy

The declarer is the member of the partnership winning the auction who first suggested the denomination of the contract. This isn't necessarily the last player to bid. In our example, South is the declarer, since South first suggested spades as the trump suit. If the partnership had ended up in a contract with clubs as the trump suit, it would be North who would be the declarer because North was the first to mention clubs.

The declarer plays both of the partnership hands once the opening lead is made. Declarer will try to make the contract for the partnership.

The cards in declarer's partner's hand are referred to as the dummy. Once the opening lead is made, North's entire hand is placed face up on the table as the dummy. South, as declarer, will now choose the cards to be played from the dummy to each trick.

The Opening Lead

The opening lead is always made by the player to the left of the declarer. In our sample auction, this would be West because South is the declarer. West selects a card and places it face up on the table. North then puts down the dummy, and the play starts.

The Defenders

With South as the declarer, East and West become the defenders, or *opponents*. As a partnership, they're trying to take enough tricks to prevent declarer from successfully making the contract. If declarer is trying to take ten of the thirteen tricks to make the 4♠ contract, the defenders need to take at least four tricks to defeat the contract.

Summary

After the cards have been dealt, the auction begins with dealer. Each player in turn, clockwise around the table, has an opportunity to bid or pass. The auction ends following a bid when the next three players say "Pass." The last bid becomes the contract.

Each bid consists of a number from one to seven followed by a denomination. The number represents the number of tricks the partnership is committing to take in addition to the required book of six tricks. The denomination is the suggested suit or notrump in which the contract would be played. The denominations are ranked with clubs as the lowest, followed by diamonds, hearts, spades, and notrump as the highest. Each bid must be higher than the previous bid. To suggest a lower ranking denomination than the previous bid, you must move up a level.

When the auction is complete, the declarer is the player who first mentioned the denomination of the contract for the partnership which won the auction. The player to the left of declarer makes the opening lead. Declarer's partner puts down the entire hand as dummy, and the play commences. Declarer plays both hands for the partnership and tries to make the contract. The other partnership tries to defeat the contract.

Points are awarded for bidding and making contracts. There's a game bonus awarded for reaching specific levels in each denomination. The minimum levels for the game bonus in each denomination are 3NT, 4♥, 4♠, 5♣, and 5♦. There are also bonuses for bidding and making a small slam—twelve tricks—or a grand slam—thirteen tricks. The defense receives points if the contract is defeated.

Exercises

1. The auction goes like this:

WEST	NORTH	EAST	SOUTH
	Pass	1♦	1♠
2♥	2♠	3♦	Pass
3♥	Pass	4♥	Pass
Pass	Pass		

a) Which player was the dealer? *N*
b) Which player was the opening bidder? *E*
c) What is the contract? *4 H*
d) Which player is the declarer? *W*
e) Which player's hand is the dummy? *E*
f) Which player makes the opening lead? *N*
g) Which players are the defenders? *N/S*
h) What's the trump suit? *H*
i) How many tricks must declarer take to make the contract? *10*
j) How many tricks must the defenders take to defeat the contract? *4*
k) What will be the trick score if declarer takes the required number of tricks? *120*
l) Will there be a game bonus if the contract is successful? *Yes*
m) Which side will get points if declarer takes eight tricks? *opponents*
   N/S

2. The auction goes like this:

WEST	NORTH	EAST	SOUTH
		Pass	Pass
Pass	1♦	2♣	2♦
2♥	2NT	Pass	Pass
Pass			

a) Which player was the dealer? *E*
b) Which player was the opening bidder? *N*
c) What's the contract? *2NT*
d) Which player is the declarer? *N*
e) Which player's hand is the dummy? *S*
f) Which player makes the opening lead? *E*
g) Which players are the defenders? *E + W*
h) What's the denomination of the contract? *NT*
i) How many tricks must declarer take to make the contract? *8*
j) How many tricks must the defenders take to defeat the contract? *6*
k) What will be the trick score if declarer takes the required number of tricks? *70 (40 + 30)*
l) Will there be a game bonus if the contract is successful? *No*
m) Which side will get points if declarer takes eight tricks? *N/S*

Answers to Exercises

1a) North. The dealer speaks first. North started the auction by passing.

1b) East. East opened the bidding 1♦.

1c) 4♥. The last bid of 4♥ was followed by three passes.

1d) West. West was the player who first bid hearts for the partnership.

1e) East. Declarer's partner, East, will put down the dummy.

1f) North. North is the player to declarer's left.

1g) North-South are the defenders.

1h) Hearts. The trump suit is the denomination named in the contract.

1i) Ten. A contract of 4♥ requires the book of six tricks plus four more tricks.

1j) Four. The defenders need to take four or more of the thirteen tricks to prevent declarer from taking ten tricks.

1k) 120 points. The trick score for hearts is 30 points per trick.

1l) Yes. The trick score of 120 points is more than the 100 points required for a game bonus.

1m) North-South. If declarer takes only eight tricks, North-South will have defeated the contract by two tricks.

2a) East. East started the auction with a pass.

2b) North. North opened the bidding 1♦.

2c) 2NT. The bid of 2NT was followed by three passes.

2d) North. North was the first player to bid notrump.

2e) South. North's partner, South, puts the hand down as dummy.

2f) East. East is the player on declarer's (North's) left.

2g) East-West are the defenders.

2h) Notrump. The contract will be played without a trump suit.

2i) Eight. A contract of 2NT requires the book of six tricks plus two more.

2j) **Six**. The defenders will need to take six or more tricks to defeat the 2NT contract.

2k) **70 points**. The trick score for notrump contracts is 40 points for the first trick plus 30 points for each subsequent trick.

2l) **No**. A contract of 2NT is a partscore contract because the trick score is worth fewer than 100 points.

2m) **North-South**. Eight tricks are all that are required to fulfill the contract.

Hand Valuation

"I know a trick worth two of that."

—WILLIAM SHAKESPEARE,
Henry IV

You're driving in the country, when in the distance you spot many cars parked along the side of the road. As you get closer, you can see that it's an antique auction. To participate in a meaningful way, you'd have to know the value of the items being auctioned and how much you could afford to spend. In a bridge auction, some contracts are more valuable than others. A contract of 3NT offers a chance for a game bonus, while a less valuable contract, 3♣, doesn't. The next step is to know to what level your partnership can afford to bid. Let's see how the partnership does this.

The Point-Count Method

You start by making an estimate of the trick-taking potential of your hand. This is made easier by using the Point-Count method of evaluation developed by Milton Work and popularized by Charles Goren in the late forties. It's the standard method used by bridge players around the world.

The Value of High Cards

How are tricks won? The first thing that comes to mind is the high cards—aces and kings win tricks. In the Point-Count method, the four highest cards in each suit are assigned a value based on their relative trick-taking potential. The scale that's universally used is:

High Card Points

Ace	4 points
King	3 points
Queen	2 points
Jack	1 point

HCP

These are called *high card points*, commonly abbreviated as *HCPs*. There are a total of 10 HCPs available in each suit. The total number of HCPs in the deck is 40.

Suppose you're dealt the following hand:

♠ K 10 8 5	3 points
♥ A 9	4 points
♦ Q J 8 2	3 points
♣ K J 4	4 points

This hand has a total of 14 high card points.

For practice, count the high card points held by each of the players in the following deal. Notice that the total HCPs adds up to 40.

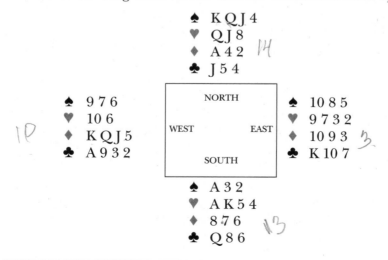

North
♠ K Q J 4
♥ Q J 8
♦ A 4 2 *14*
♣ J 5 4

West
♠ 9 7 6
♥ 10 6
♦ K Q J 5
♣ A 9 3 2
10

East
♠ 10 8 5
♥ 9 7 3 2
♦ 10 9 3 *3*
♣ K 10 7

South
♠ A 3 2
♥ A K 5 4
♦ 8 7 6 *13*
♣ Q 8 6

Here are the totals:

North	14
East	3
South	13
West	10
Total HCPs	40

The Value of Long Suits

High cards aren't the only source of tricks. The low cards from long suits can sometimes take tricks once the high cards have been played. To reflect this, the Point-Count method takes into consideration the long suits you hold, using the following scale for *length points*:

Length Points	
5-card suit	1 point
6-card suit	2 points
7-card suit	3 points
8-card suit	4 points

Suppose you're dealt the following hand:

♠ 10 8 7 6 4 2
♥ 9 6 5 3 2
♦ 4
♣ 2

Although there are no high cards, the hand still has some value based on the long suits. You can count 2 points for the six-card spade suit and 1 point for the five-card heart suit, giving the hand a total value of 3 points.*

---

*Some players prefer giving value to the short suits in a hand, rather than the long suits. This usually works out about the same, but I suggest that you use the above scale when starting out. We'll take a look at the value of short suits later on.

Summing Up

The total value of your hand is a combination of the high card points and the length points. For example, suppose you have this hand:

♠ A K 8 6 5 2
♥ A 7 4   14
♦ J 9 5
♣ 7

There are 12 high card points: 4 for the ♠A; 3 for the ♠K; 4 for the ♥A; 1 for the ♦J. There are also 2 length points for the six-card spade suit. That gives you a total of 14 points as the value of the hand.

For practice, value the hands held by each of the players in the following deal:

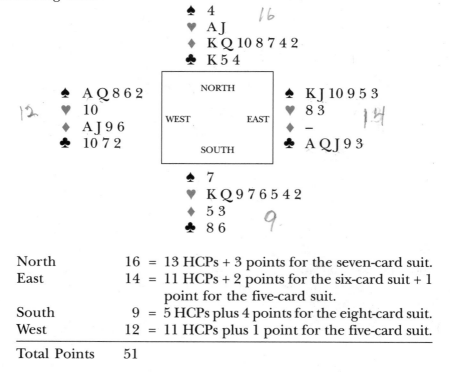

North	16 = 13 HCPs + 3 points for the seven-card suit.
East	14 = 11 HCPs + 2 points for the six-card suit + 1 point for the five-card suit.
South	9 = 5 HCPs plus 4 points for the eight-card suit.
West	12 = 11 HCPs plus 1 point for the five-card suit.
Total Points	51

When the value of long suits is taken into account, there can be more than 40 total points among the four hands.

Two Pieces of the Puzzle

During the auction, the partnership has to decide on two things:

- The level at which the partnership belongs: partscore, game, or slam.
- The denomination in which the partnership should play: clubs, diamonds, hearts, spades, or notrump.

The Level—Translating Points into Tricks

The usefulness of the Point Count method is that there's a relationship between points and tricks. A partnership with no combined points could be expected to take no tricks. A partnership with all 40 high card points could be expected to take all of the tricks. Experience has shown that about 26 points between the two hands will produce nine tricks in a notrump contract or ten tricks in a suit contract—because of the added value of the trump suit. Since there's a game bonus awarded for bidding and making a contract of 3NT, 4♥, or 4♠, the partnership can use the following guidelines:

- With 26 or more combined points, play at least at a game contract of 3NT, 4♥, or 4♠.
- With fewer than 26 combined points, play in a partscore contract.

What about the game bonus contracts of 5♣ and 5♦? These require eleven tricks, and the partnership would need about 29 combined points to take that many tricks. As a result, the partnership focuses on reaching a contract of 3NT, 4♥, or 4♠ when there are about 26 combined points. Rarely does the partnership consider playing in a 5♣ or 5♦ contract—and then only with some extra strength.

There are extra bonuses for bidding a slam. These are infrequent, but the partnership can use the following guidelines:

- With 33 or more combined points, play in any small slam contract (6♣, 6♦, 6♥, 6♠, or 6NT).
- With 37 or more combined points, play in any grand slam contract (7♣, 7♦, 7♥, 7♠, or 7NT).

As you'll see in the upcoming chapters, the partnership is usually focused on finding out whether or not it has the 26 combined points required to reach a game contract.

Finding a Fit

The second thing the partnership has to decide is whether to play the hand with a trump suit or in notrump. There are advantages to playing with a trump suit because the low cards in the trump suit can be used to win tricks. That works both ways, however. The other partnership can also take advantage of the trump suit to try to win tricks.

To choose one suit as the trump suit during the auction, your side wants to have the most combined cards in the suit. There are thirteen cards in each suit. If your side is to have the majority of the cards in the trump suit, you need to have at least seven cards between the two hands. Does this sound familiar? Seven is also the minimum number of tricks you need to win to take more than the average number of tricks available.

The number of cards held in a suit between the partnership hands is referred to as the *fit*. It's more comfortable to have at least eight cards between the two hands—an eight-card fit—to choose the suit as the trump suit. That leaves the other side with no more than five. Bridge writers often refer to a holding of eight or more combined cards in a suit as a "magic" or "golden" fit because it's so useful as a trump suit.

Much of the language of bidding centers around finding a suitable trump fit. If the partnership has a suitable fit, it will try to make that suit the trump suit. Otherwise, the partnership will want to play in notrump.

To get a feeling for eight-card fits, take one suit from the deck of cards and try dividing up eight cards between the North and South hands.

They can be divided in many different patterns. The most extreme would be for one player to have all eight cards and the other player to have no cards in the suit. Imagine the auction! One player would be raving about the suit, and the other would be trying to warn partner away from the suit. That would be the kind of division that builds partnership trust.

If the cards are divided more evenly, communication during the auction will be more straightforward. North and South might each have four cards in a suit. They would both like the suit, and the total would be an eight-card fit. One player could have six cards in the suit and the other two. Frequently, one player has five cards in the suit, and the other has three. All in all, whatever the division, if the total number of cards held by the partnership is eight or more, there's a suitable trump fit.

You can also see what happens as you divide the remaining cards in the suit between the other two hands. In the worst case, one hand holds all five of the trumps. That could make things a little awkward during the play. That's why it's often better to have more than eight combined cards in your trump suit. Most of the time, even if you have only eight combined cards, the remaining five will be divided three and two between the other partnership's hands.

There's one other consideration when it comes to finding a trump fit in the partnership hands: major suit fits are more important than minor suit fits. Although it doesn't make much difference which suit is the trump suit when you play at the partscore level or the slam level, it makes a big difference at the game level. The bonus level contracts of 4♥ and 4♠ require only ten tricks, whereas the contracts of 5♣ and 5♦ require declarer to take eleven tricks. As a result, the partnership will continue to look for a major suit fit during the auction, even if it has already found a minor suit fit. More on that later.

Hand Shape

A bridge hand is often described according to its *shape,* or *pattern.* This is related to the number of cards held in each suit. There's a special vocabulary associated with suits in which you don't hold many cards:

- A *void* is zero cards in a suit.
- A *singleton* is one card in a suit.
- A *doubleton* is two cards in a suit.

In this hand, you have a singleton spade and a doubleton diamond:

♠ 3
♥ K Q 9 8 5
♦ 10 3
♣ A Q J 8 5

Bridge players also use the terms "balanced" and "unbalanced" to describe the overall shape of a hand.

Balanced Hands

A *balanced hand* is a hand which contains no voids, no singletons, and at most one doubleton. There are three balanced hand patterns possible with the thirteen cards. Ideally, the most balanced hand possible would consist of three cards in each suit, but that would be only twelve cards. Each hand has to have at least one four-card or longer suit.

Here are the balanced hand patterns. The particular cards in each suit and the order of the suits aren't relevant at this point. The shape is the focus. If you want to get a better feel for hand patterns, lay out thirteen cards face down on the table as follows.

X X X X
X X X
X X X
X X X

This pattern is referred to as 4-3-3-3. The numbers represent the number of cards in each suit. There are no voids, no singletons, and no doubletons in the hand. It fits the definition of a balanced hand pattern. Here's the second hand pattern that fits the definition:

X X X X
X X X X
X X X
X X

This hand shape is called 4-4-3-2. There are two four-card suits, one three-card suit, and one doubleton. There's only one doubleton, so the hand fits into the definition. The final balanced hand pattern is the following.

```
x  x  x  x  x
x  x  x
x  x  x
x  x
```

This hand shape is referred to as 5-3-3-2. There's a five-card suit, two three-card suits, and one doubleton.

If you try arranging the thirteen cards into different patterns, you'll see that these are the only three possible balanced hand shapes. Any other distribution of the cards among the four suits will result in a void, a singleton, or more than one doubleton.

Unbalanced Hands

All hands that don't fit the definition of a balanced distribution of the suits are considered *unbalanced*. There are many possible unbalanced hand patterns. An extremely unbalanced hand would have thirteen cards in one suit and three voids in the other suits—although the chance of that happening is very rare. Most unbalanced hands don't involve such wild distribution. This would be a more typical unbalanced hand:

```
x  x  x  x  x  x
x  x  x  x
x  x
x
```

The shape of this hand would be referred to as 6-4-2-1. Because it has a singleton, it's considered unbalanced.

Remember, it's the distribution of the suits within the hand that determines whether or not a hand is balanced—not the actual cards in each suit. See if you can spot the balanced and unbalanced hands from this complete deal:

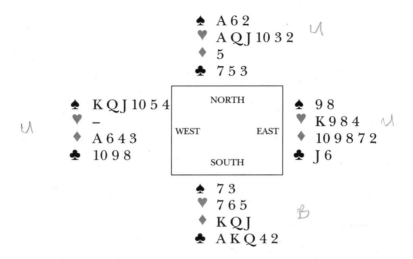

♠ A 6 2
♥ A Q J 10 3 2
♦ 5
♣ 7 5 3

	NORTH	
♠ K Q J 10 5 4		♠ 9 8
♥ —	WEST EAST	♥ K 9 8 4
♦ A 6 4 3		♦ 10 9 8 7 2
♣ 10 9 8	SOUTH	♣ J 6

♠ 7 3
♥ 7 6 5
♦ K Q J
♣ A K Q 4 2

North's hand is unbalanced because it contains a singleton. Its shape would be described as 6-3-3-1: a six-card suit, two three-card suits, and a singleton.

East's hand is also unbalanced. Its shape is 5-4-2-2 and is considered unbalanced because there are two doubletons.

South holds a balanced hand, 5-3-3-2. There are no singletons or voids and only one doubleton.

West's hand pattern is 6-4-3-0. That's definitely unbalanced, since it contains a void.

Balanced hands are generally more suitable to play in notrump, and unbalanced hands are more suitable to play with one suit as the trump suit. It's the combined partnership holdings that are important, however, when it comes to deciding on the best contract. Unless there's a suitable trump fit, the partnership will usually end up playing in a notrump contract, even when one or both hands are unbalanced. For now, when you pick up your hand, notice both the strength—in terms of the Point-Count—and the shape. These are the characteristics that, through the language of bidding, you're going to describe to your partner.

Summary

Hands can be valued using the Point-Count method, which gives points to the high cards and long suits using the following scale:

High Card Points		Length Points	
Ace	4 points	5-card suit	1 point
King	3 points	6-card suit	2 points
Queen	2 points	7-card suit	3 points
Jack	1 point	8-card suit	4 points

Hands can also be classified as balanced or unbalanced. A balanced hand contains no voids or singletons and at most one doubleton. All other hand patterns are unbalanced.

During the auction, the partnership exchanges information about the strength and distribution of the hands. They use the following guidelines when deciding on the contract:

- With fewer than 26 combined points, the partnership should play in a partscore contract.
- With 26 or more combined points, the partnership should play at least at game contract (3NT, 4♥, or 4♠).
- With 33 or more combined points, the partnership should play in any small slam contract (6♣, 6♦, 6♥, 6♠, or 6NT).
- With 37 or more combined points, the partnership should play in any grand slam contract (7♣, 7♦, 7♥, 7♠, or 7NT).
- To choose a suit as a trump suit, the partnership should have an eight-card or longer fit. Major suit fits are more important than minor suit fits. Without a major suit, game contracts are usually played in 3NT rather than 5♣ or 5♦.

Exercises

1. What's the Point-Count value of each of the following hands?

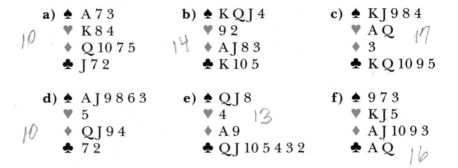

a) ♠ A 7 3
♥ K 8 4
♦ Q 10 7 5
♣ J 7 2

10

b) ♠ K Q J 4
♥ 9 2
♦ A J 8 3
♣ K 10 5

14

c) ♠ K J 9 8 4
♥ A Q
♦ 3
♣ K Q 10 9 5

17

d) ♠ A J 9 8 6 3
♥ 5
♦ Q J 9 4
♣ 7 2

10

e) ♠ Q J 8
♥ 4
♦ A 9
♣ Q J 10 5 4 3 2

13

f) ♠ 9 7 3
♥ K J 5
♦ A J 10 9 3
♣ A Q

16

2. Which of the above hands are balanced? *A, B, F*

3. If your partner has a hand worth 18 points, what target level (partscore, game, slam) should the partnership be aiming for when you hold a hand of the following value?

a) 5 points **b)** 10 points **c)** 15 points **d)** 20 points
partscore   *game*   *small slam*   *grand slam*

8 total

4. To choose hearts as the trump suit, how many hearts do you need in your hand when partner shows the following number of hearts?

a) Two hearts **b)** Four hearts **c)** Five hearts **d)** Six hearts
6   *4*   *3*   *2*

Answers to Exercises

1a) **10.** 4 for the ♠A, 3 for the ♥K, 2 for the ♦Q, and 1 for the ♣J.

1b) **14.** 6 HCPs in spades, 5 in diamonds, and 3 in clubs.

1c) **17.** 4 HCPs in spades, 6 HCPs in hearts, 5 HCPs in clubs, 1 length point for the five-card spade suit, and 1 length point for the five-card club suit.

1d) **10.** 8 HCPs plus 2 points for the six-card spade suit.

1e) **13.** 10 HCPs plus 3 points for the seven-card suit.

1f) **16.** 15 HCPs plus 1 length point for the five-card diamond suit.

2a) **Balanced.** This is a 4-3-3-3 pattern.

2b) **Balanced.** This hand has 4-4-3-2 shape.

2c) **Unbalanced.** The 5-5-2-1 pattern includes a singleton.

2d) **Unbalanced.** The 6-4-2-1 shape includes a singleton.

2e) **Unbalanced.** 7-3-2-1 is an unbalanced hand pattern.

2f) **Balanced.** This hand is 5-3-3-2. There are no voids or singletons and only one doubleton.

3a) **Partscore.** The combined strength is only 23 points.

3b) **Game.** There are 28 combined points, more than enough for a game contract.

3c) **Slam.** There are 33 combined points, enough for a small slam.

3d) **Slam.** There are 38 combined points, enough for a grand slam.

4a) **Six.** You need six hearts to give the partnership a combined total of eight.

4b) **Four.** Four hearts in both hands gives the partnership an eight-card fit.

4c) **Three.** Five plus three equals eight.

4d) **Two.** Six and two make up an eight-card fit.

Making the
First Bid

"Of a good beginning cometh a good end."
—JOHN HEYWOOD,
Proverbs [1546]

Someone has to get the auction started by making an opening bid. A bridge auction always proceeds in an orderly manner. The dealer gets the first opportunity to open the bidding. If the dealer passes, the auction moves clockwise around the table until someone opens the bidding. If everyone passes, there's no auction, and it's time to deal a new hand.

Most auctions begin at the one level, although there are some hands where the opening bid is at the two level or higher. An opening bid, such as 1♦ or 1♠, is a commitment for the partnership to take at least seven of the thirteen tricks—the "book" of six tricks plus the number of tricks bid. That's more than half the available tricks. What sort of hand do you need to get the bidding started for your side? Let's take a look.

Starting at the One Level

It might seem as though you need more than half of the 40 available high card points to open the bidding at the one level because you're now committed to take more than half the tricks. If that were the case, you would wait a long time before anyone opened the bidding. Hands of 20 or more points aren't that common. Bridge is a partnership game, however, and it's the combined strength of the hands that will be important. You don't have to take the tricks all by yourself.

Instead, you need a better than average hand to start the auction. If the high cards were evenly divided around the table, everyone would have 10 high card points—an ace, a king, a queen, and a jack. To start the bidding at the one level, it's generally accepted that you need the equivalent of an extra king, or 13 points in total. With fewer than that, you should pass and hope that your partner can start the auction. Usually, someone at the table will hold 13 or more points.

There's an accepted upper limit of about 21 points for opening bids at the one level. Putting a limit on the range of strength for an opening bid helps determine the combined strength of the hands. If you open the bidding at the one level, partner can assume that you have a hand in the range of 13 to 21 points. We'll see a little later on what you do with more than 21 points.

In summary, when you have an opportunity to open the bidding, you can use the following guideline:

- With fewer than 13 points, pass.
- With 13 to 21 points, open the bidding at the one level.

It's not too difficult to remember that you need 13 or more points to open the bidding at the one level. There are 13 cards in each suit and 13 cards in each hand. 13 is an important number in the game of bridge!

Another way of thinking about opening the bidding is to remember that the partnership needs about 26 combined points to go for the game bonus contracts of 3NT, 4♥, or 4♠. If neither partner opens the bidding with 13 or more points, the partnership would miss the opportunity to bid and make a game level contract.

Bidding a Suit

One of the things the partnership is trying to do during the auction is to find a good trump suit. The partnership wants to find a suit that has eight or more combined cards. Since it's unlikely that one partner will hold an eight-card suit, the partnership must work together during the auction to uncover its fits. In general, the best way to start this process is for the opening bidder to start by bidding the longest suit in the hand. Suppose you pick up this hand. You're the dealer and have the first chance to make a call:

♠ K 3
♥ Q J 9 7 5
♦ A K 8 4
♣ 6 4

You have 13 high card points plus 1 point for the five-card suit. That's enough to open the bidding. You want to start off by telling partner about the longest suit in your hand, hearts. To do this, you would open the bidding 1♥. Hearts isn't the strongest suit in your hand, but it's the longest. The partnership is trying to find the longest combined suit in the two hands. Cards such as the ♦A and ♦K will probably take tricks even if hearts are the trump suit. Cards such as the ♥9, ♥7, and ♥5 are probably going to take tricks only if hearts are the trump suit. So, the general guideline for opening the bidding at the one level in a suit is:

- Bid your longest suit first.

How many cards do you need in a suit in order to suggest it as a trump suit? Thirteen is an interesting number. If you were to divide the thirteen cards in a suit among the four players at the table, each player would receive three cards, and there would be one card left over. The player who received the extra card would have a four-card suit, and this would be better than the average number of cards one could expect.

Deal out any hand. There will be at least one suit in the hand that has four or more cards. To express interest in a suit, then, you need to have at least four cards in the suit—and you hope to have more.

Here are some examples:

15

♠ K J 8 7 6 3
♥ A K J 7 5
♦ 6 4
♣ —

Open the bidding 1♠. There are 12 high card points plus 2 points for the six-card suit and 1 point for the five-card suit—a total of 15 points. That's more than enough to open the bidding at the one level. Start with your longest suit, spades. Hopefully, you'll get an opportunity to tell partner about your other suit later in the auction.

20

♠ 7 4
♥ K J
♦ A Q J 9
♣ A K J 8 7

Open the bidding 1♣, your longest suit. Although this hand is worth 20 points—19 high card points plus 1 for the five-card club suit—the opening bid is still at the one level. One level opening bids in a suit cover a wide range of strength, from about 13 to 21 points.

Pass

♠ 9 6 4
♥ Q 9 7 6 4 2
♦ K 8
♣ Q 5

Pass. There are only 7 high card points plus 2 points for the six-card suit. This is not enough to open the bidding at the one level.

13

♠ J 7 4
♥ K 9 3
♦ A 10 5
♣ K Q 6 2

Open 1♣. You have 13 high card points, and your longest suit is clubs.

Sometimes, you'll have a choice of suits to open. You can use the following guideline:

• With a choice of suits, open the higher-ranking.

♠ 8 4
♥ A K 7 4 2
♦ A K 9 6 3
♣ 3

With a choice between showing your five-card heart suit or your five-card diamond suit, bid the higher-ranking suit. Start the bidding with 1♥ because hearts are higher ranking than diamonds.

♠ K 8 3
♥ 4 2
♦ A Q 6 2
♣ A 10 8 3

Here you have a choice of four-card suits to start the auction. Bid 1♦, since diamonds rank higher than clubs.

There are many different styles that can be used by a partnership when choosing the suit to open at the one level.* The guidelines above will let you get started.

Opening 1NT

The other choice of opening bid at the one level is 1NT. By general agreement, this opening bid is used to show a very specific type of hand. It shows a balanced hand pattern—no void, no singleton, and no more than one doubleton—with the strength lying within a three point range. Typically, a range of 16 to 18 points is used, although some partnerships prefer other ranges, such as 15–17 points, 13–15 points, or even 12–14 points. The specific range is a matter of partnership agreement. Some ranges are more popular in certain areas or countries around the globe. You'll soon find out the style that's popular among the bridge players in your community. For the purpose of this book, we'll adopt the following guideline:

- An opening bid of 1NT shows a balanced hand with 16, 17, or 18 points.

Here are some examples:

♠ A 8 7
♥ K J 7
♦ Q J 10 9
♣ A J 2

In North America, this could be referred to as a textbook 1NT opening bid. The hand is balanced and has 16 high card points—falling within the range of 16, 17, or 18 points.

---

* Some partnerships use Five-Card Majors, where an opening bid of 1♥ or 1♠ shows a five-card or longer suit. Methods such as this are covered in the second book in this series, *Better Bridge—Bidding*.

♠ K Q 9 4　　　　　Open 1NT. This is a balanced hand—no
♥ A Q　　　　　　voids or singletons and only one doubleton—
♦ K 10 9　　　　　and there are 17 high card points. That makes
♣ K 10 5 2　　　　it ideal for a 1NT opening bid.

Priorities

The 1NT opening bid is very descriptive, since it tells partner a lot about both your strength and distribution. Bids that describe the strength of a hand within a narrow range of points are called *limit bids*. Although opening bids of 1♣, 1♦, 1♥, and 1♠ do have a lower and upper limit, the range is too great—13–21 points—for them to be considered limit bids.

It's always a good idea to make a limit bid whenever possible because it gives your partner an accurate description of the hand. With a choice of opening the bidding in one-of-a-suit or 1NT, prefer to open 1NT. The rest of the auction will be much easier for the partnership, as you'll see in the next chapter. Consider this hand:

♠ A J 5
♥ Q 8
♦ K Q 10 8 6
♣ K J 9

You have 16 high card points plus 1 for the five-card diamond suit. The hand is also balanced, with no singletons or voids and only one doubleton. You might think about starting the bidding with 1♦, showing your long suit. This wouldn't paint the most accurate picture of your hand for partner. For a 1♦ opening bid, you could have anywhere from 13 to 21 points, and you could have a balanced hand or a very unbalanced hand—with six diamonds and five clubs perhaps. Partner will have only a vague idea of what your hand looks like.

It's better to open the bidding 1NT with this hand, giving priority to the accurate description of both your strength and distribution. Partner will know right away that you have 16, 17, or 18 points and that your hand falls into one of the three balanced shapes: 4-3-3-3, 4-4-3-2, or 5-3-3-2. The bidding conversation will not take very long once partner has all this information from your first bid.

Let's look at some other examples of opening bids, keeping in mind that 1NT takes priority.

♠ A 8
♥ K J 6
♦ K 9 5
♣ K J 9 8 4

Open 1NT. There are only 15 high card points, but you can add 1 point for the five-card club suit, putting you in the range for 1NT. The hand is balanced, with no voids or singletons and only one doubleton.

♠ A 8
♥ K J 6
♦ J 9 5
♣ K J 9 8 4

Open 1♣. This hand looks similar to the previous one because it's still a balanced hand. There are only 14 points, however—13 high card points plus 1 for the five-card suit. That's not enough strength to open the bidding 1NT.

Instead, start with the longest suit, clubs. You have to wait to show your balanced distribution until later in the auction.

♠ A 8
♥ K J 6
♦ A Q 5
♣ K J 9 8 4

Open 1♣. This time, the hand is too strong to open the bidding 1NT because it contains 19 points—18 high card points plus 1 for the five-card suit. Open your longest suit. Hopefully, you'll get a chance to show your strength later in the bidding conversation.

♠ A 8
♥ K J 6 5 4
♦ K 9
♣ K J 9 8

Open 1♥. The hand is worth 16 points— 15 high card points plus 1 for the five-card suit—but it's not balanced, since there are two doubletons. Open the longest suit, hearts.

Higher Level Opening Bids

Although the bidding is usually opened at the one level, there are some hands which are opened at the two level or higher.

Two-level Bids in a Suit

Unbalanced hands with 22 or more points are opened at the two level, rather than the one level. This sends the message to partner that you pretty well have enough strength to commit to a game level contract all by yourself. If partner does have some strength, the partnership may well belong at the slam level. For example:

♠ A K 4 3
♥ A K J 10 9 8
♦ A 3
♣ A

This hand has 23 high card points plus 2 for the six-card suit. It's likely that your side will be able to make a game level contract even if partner has only 1 or 2 points. Open 2♥, rather than 1♥. As you'll see later, this tells partner that you want the auction to keep going until at least the game level is reached.

Strong Balanced Hands

Very strong balanced hands are opened in notrump at the two level or higher. You can use the following guidelines:

- An opening bid of 2NT shows a balanced hand with 22, 23, or 24 points.
- An opening bid of 3NT shows a balanced hand with 25, 26, or 27 points.

If you keep getting hands with 28 or more points, let me know—I want to be your partner! Here are two examples of higher level notrump opening bids:

♠ K Q 8 *22*   Open 2NT. This is a balanced hand with 22
♥ A Q J   *2NT* high card points.
♦ K Q 9 4 *(22-24)*
♣ A J 7

♠ A K   *26*   Open 3NT. This is a balanced hand with 26
♥ K J 10   *3NT* high card points.
♦ A K Q 8 *(25-27)*
♣ K Q J 7

Three-level Opening Bids in a Suit

Since opening bids in a suit at the one level cover hands of about 13 to 21 points, and opening bids at the two level are used for hands with 22 or more points, there doesn't appear to be much use for opening bids at the three level in a suit. Perhaps surprisingly, these are used to show hands containing long suits that are too weak to open at the one level!

Here's a typical example:

♠ 9 6   *9*
♥ 5
♦ K Q J 9 8 6 5
♣ 7 3 2

This hand would be opened 3♦. This is called a *preemptive opening bid.* A discussion of the theory behind preemptive bids is beyond the scope of this book, but the basic idea is to make the auction more difficult for the opponents while describing a specific type of hand to partner. A preemptive opening bid generally shows a good seven-card or longer suit with less than the values for an opening bid at the one level.

With the above hand, you can tell partner that your hand is suitable for play only if diamonds are the trump suit. At the same time, you don't leave much room in the auction for the opponents to have a bidding conversation to try to reach their best contract.

With very long suits, preemptive opening bids are sometimes made at the four level or higher. They're an exciting part of the game but are best left until you've had lots of practice with the more mundane hands the partnership has to deal with.

Summary

The dealer has the first opportunity to open the bidding. If the dealer passes, the opportunity to start the auction moves clockwise around the table. When you have an opportunity to open the bidding, use the following guidelines:

With fewer than 13 points, pass.

With 13 to 21 points:

- Open the bidding 1NT with a balanced hand and 16–18 points.
- Otherwise, open the bidding at the one level in your longest suit. With a choice of equal-length suits, open the higher-ranking.

With 22 or more points:

- Open the bidding 2NT with a balanced hand and 22–24 points.
- Open the bidding 3NT with a balanced hand and 25–27 points.
- Otherwise, open the bidding at the two level in your longest suit. With a choice of equal-length suits, open the higher-ranking.

Exercises

1. You have an opportunity to open the bidding. What would you do with each of the following hands?

Pass

a) ♠ KJ8   *1D*
  ♥ 4
  ♦ AQ 10 875 *14*
  ♣ Q42
    1D

b) ♠ AJ7   *1NT*
  ♥ KQ9 *16*
  ♦ J84
  ♣ KQ 10 5
    1NT

c) ♠ J984
  ♥ AJ63
  ♦ 3
  ♣ Q975
    Pass

d) ♠ AJ 10 72 *1S*
  ♥ 94
  ♦ KQJ 10 6 *13*
  ♣ 2
    1 S

e) ♠ QJ3 *1NT*
  ♥ Q2 *18*
  ♦ AQ82
  ♣ AK76
    1NT

f) ♠ 1084 *1D*
  ♥ AQ6 *13*
  ♦ KJ93
  ♣ K64
    1D

g) ♠ AK763 *1C*
  ♥ 4 *14*
  ♦ 5
  ♣ KJ 10 842
    1C

h) ♠ K 10 5 *1NT*
  ♥ K7 *17*
  ♦ QJ3
  ♣ AQJ83
    1NT

i) ♠ AK6
  ♥ KQ *20 1D*
  ♦ AQ87
  ♣ Q 10 63
    1 D

j) ♠ AKQJ6 *2S*
  ♥ KQJ4
  ♦ 5 *24*
  ♣ AQJ
    2 S

k) ♠ KQJ *23*
  ♥ AQ6 *2c*
  ♦ AK8
  ♣ KJ 10 8
    23
    2NT

l) ♠ 84
  ♥ 8 *11*
  ♦ 532 *pass*
  ♣ AKJ9754
    11
    pass
    3 C (preemptive)

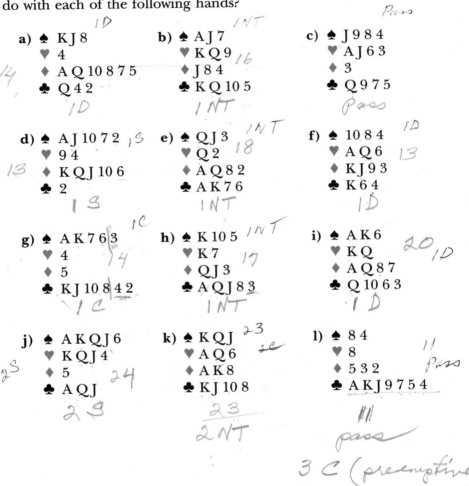

Answers to Exercises

1a) **1♦**. There are 12 high card points plus 2 length points for the six-card diamond suit. Open the bidding in your longest suit.

1b) **1NT**. This a balanced hand with 16 HCPs. The hand falls into the range for the descriptive opening bid of 1NT.

1c) **Pass**. There are only 8 HCPs. That's not enough strength to open the bidding.

1d) **1♠**. The hand is worth 13 points—11 HCPs plus 1 point for each of the five-card suits. With a choice of five-card suits, open the higher-ranking.

1e) **1NT**. The 4-4-3-2 shape is balanced, and there are 18 HCPs.

1f) **1♦**. Although the hand is balanced, there are only 13 HCPs. Open the longest suit.

1g) **1♣**. There are 11 HCPs plus 2 points for the six-card suit and 1 point for the five-card suit—a total of 14 points. Open the bidding in the longer of your two suits.

1h) **1NT**. The hand is worth 17 points—16 HCPs plus 1 for the five-card suit. With a balanced hand pattern of 5-3-3-2, open the bidding 1NT.

1i) **1♦**. The hand is balanced, but there are 20 HCPs, too much for an opening bid of 1NT. Instead, open the higher-ranking of your two four-card suits.

1j) **2♠**. The hand is worth 24 points—23 HCPs plus 1 for the five-card suit. With an unbalanced hand of 22 or more points, open at the two level in your longest suit.

1k) **2NT**. With a balanced hand of 23 points, open with the descriptive bid of 2NT.

1l) **3♣** (or Pass). With only 8 HCPs plus 3 points for the seven-card suit, you don't have enough strength for an opening bid at the one level. The hand could be opened with a preemptive bid in a suit at the three level, showing a good seven-card suit with less than the values for an opening bid. Alternatively, you could pass and hope to show your long suit later in the auction.

Responding— A First Look

"It is better to know some of the questions than all
of the answers."

—JAMES THURBER

Two people are having a conversation about what to have for dinner. One person starts off with a suggestion: "I'd like to eat at
Winston's tonight; if we get there before seven o'clock, it won't be
crowded, and they have special early-bird prices. What do you think?"
You may or may not like the suggestion, but you have been given
some information and asked to participate in making a decision.
You'll respond to the suggestion, and the conversation should carry
on smoothly. Bidding conversations are similar.

Opener starts the bidding conversation by suggesting playing in a
suit or in notrump. The partner of the opening bidder is called the
responder. Responder replies to opener's suggestion, using the language of bidding.

The General Idea

During the auction, the partnership wants to come to an agreement on both the level for the contract and whether the contract should be played in a suit or in notrump. The partners can't see the cards in each other's hand and must exchange enough information about the strength and distribution of the hands to come to a reasonable conclusion.

Compare this to the conversation about where to have dinner; eventually, one person makes a decision, and the other person agrees. In bridge, one member of the partnership has to take on the role of captain, making the final decision on the contract. Otherwise, the bidding could go on and on. The role of captain will go to the player who knows more about the combined hands. We'll discuss which player becomes the captain later on. For now, let's look at what the captain considers.

Deciding the Level

The captain focuses on reaching a bonus level whenever possible. This is where the partnership can score the most points. To use a baseball analogy, suppose the player up to bat hits the ball over the fence but only runs to first base. The player would be safe but wouldn't have made the most of the opportunity. The same holds true in bridge. If the partnership has enough combined strength to try for a game level contract, it would be a waste to stop and play in a partscore contract.

The captain can decide whether the partnership belongs at the game level by adding up the points in both hands to see if there are 26 or more. With fewer than 26 combined points, the partnership should stop in partscore because it's unlikely there will be enough strength to win the required tricks. With 26 or more points, the partnership should play at the game level.

The game bonus contracts 3NT, 4♥, and 4♠ require about 26 combined points. The game bonus contracts of 5♣ and 5♦ require about 29 or more points. The captain, therefore, usually focuses on reaching 3NT, 4♥, or 4♠ when there are known to be at least 26 combined points.

If the captain thinks there are 33 or more combined points, the partnership should be headed for a small slam contract. With 37 or more points, the partnership should go for the grand prize, a grand slam.

How does the captain know how many points partner holds? During the auction, one of the partners will usually end up describing the strength of the hand within some limited range. The other partner can then determine the approximate combined strength and take on the role of captain.

As an example, suppose your partner opens the bidding 1NT, showing a hand with 16, 17, or 18 points. You have just become captain! You can assume partner has about 17 points, and add that to the number of points in your hand. You know the combined strength of the two hands. It won't always be that easy, but you get the general idea.

Deciding the Denomination

The other decision the captain has to make is whether to play the contract in a trump fit or in notrump. This is similar to adding together the points in the combined hands except that you add together the cards in each suit. If a partnership has eight or more combined cards, that's a suitable trump suit.

Here's the challenge of the game. You can't see the cards held by your partner. You get a picture of the length of the suits from the bids made during the auction. For example, if partner bids 1♥, you can assume partner holds at least a four-card suit. If you also hold four hearts, you know the partnership has an eight-card or longer fit. You have found a trump suit.

If the partnership can't uncover a suitable trump suit, the captain usually places the contract in notrump. Even when an eight-card or longer minor suit fit is available as a trump suit, a notrump contract may be preferable. This is especially the case when it comes to going for the game bonus. It's usually a lot easier to take nine tricks in a contract of 3NT than eleven tricks in a contract of 5♣ or 5♦. When the partnership is headed for the game level, the captain will usually place the contract in 3NT even though there's a minor suit fit.

Responding to One Notrump

When you're learning the game, it may seem that the player who has the stronger hand should be making the decisions for the partnership during the auction. This isn't the case. It's the player who knows more about the combined hands who's in charge and takes on the role of captain. This may be the player with the weaker hand. Bridge truly is a partnership game.

Nowhere is this clearer than when the opening bid is 1NT. Opener has painted a very accurate picture of both the strength and distribution of the hand. Opener has limited the strength of the hand to the narrow range of 16, 17, or 18 points. Opener has also said that the hand is balanced: 4-3-3-3, 4-4-3-2, or 5-3-3-2. No voids, no singletons, and at most one doubleton.

It's the responder who takes on the role of captain. Responder knows a lot about opener's hand. Opener knows nothing about responder's hand. Let's see how responder makes use of the available information to lead the partnership to the best contract.

Stopping in Partscore.

Partner starts the bidding 1NT, and this is your hand:

         ♠ 3
         ♥ J 9 7 6 4 2
         ♦ 9 7 2
         ♣ 8 6 3

You might be wondering why you have to say anything when you hold a hand like this. You probably have the weakest hand at the table. That's part of the game. Partner's opening bid has put you in the role of captain, and you're going to decide on the best contract for the partnership. Let's give it a try.

You have only 3 points—1 high card point and 2 points for the length in the heart suit. You don't want to bid any higher than necessary with such limited strength. Opener has at most 18 points, so the total is no more than 21 combined points. Your first decision as captain is made. The partnership belongs in a partscore contract. There's not enough combined strength to go for a game bonus.

You would like hearts to be the trump suit. You have six of them, and partner has shown at least two by opening 1NT—partner can't have a singleton or a void. You've found an eight-card fit. Putting the pieces together, your decision is that the partnership belongs in a partscore contract with hearts as the trump suit. You send this message to partner by responding 2♥.

As you'll soon see, partner is expected to listen to your message and respect your decision to stop in partscore with hearts as the trump suit. Your 2♥ response should end the auction. Since it's the player who first mentions the trump suit who becomes the declarer, you'll be playing the hand for your side. You mentioned hearts first. You'll have to take eight tricks to make the contract, but remember partner has a good hand with 16, 17, or 18 points. You have every chance of being successful.

I have a feeling that you might not believe that it's a good idea to respond 2♥ with this hand. Try this experiment. With your deck of cards, construct the above hand for yourself, and then make up a hand for your partner that's balanced and contains about 17 points. Randomly divide the remaining cards to make up the two hands held by the defenders. Turn up all four hands. How many tricks do you think partner would take playing in a contract of 1NT? How many tricks do you think you could take playing in a contract of 2♥? I think you'll find that most of the time you won't be able to take seven tricks in a notrump contract but will be able to take eight tricks with hearts as the trump suit.

Partner has at most 18 points to open 1NT; you'll want to stop in partscore when you have 7 or fewer points. There can't be enough combined strength for a game contract. Consider these hands.

♠ 10 8 7
♥ J 4 2
♦ 8 7 6 3
♣ K 8 5

You have 4 points, so the partnership has at most 22 points between the two hands. You want to stop at the partscore level. The best thing to do is to pass. Partner will play the hand in a partscore of 1NT and try to take seven tricks.

♠ 8 6 3
♥ K J 7 4 2
♦ 3
♣ 10 8 4 2

You have 4 high card points plus 1 for the five-card suit. The partnership doesn't have enough combined strength to reach a game level contract. Partner has at least two hearts and maybe three or four, so hearts should make a reasonable trump suit. Respond 2♥. There's no guarantee of an eight-card fit when you have only a five-card suit, but you can't afford too much of a conversation when you have a weak hand. You'll have to make your best guess. After all, you're in charge.

As a guideline, when partner opens the bidding 1NT, and you have 0–7 points, bid a five-card or longer suit at the two level if you have one. Otherwise, pass, and leave the partnership in 1NT.

Going for the Bonus

Are you reading this book in private? If so, take off your shoes for a moment and wiggle your toes. This is to remind you that when partner starts the bidding with 1NT, and you have at <u>least 10</u> points, you're to take the partnership to one of the game bonus levels. Consider this hand.

♠ A 3
♥ K Q 2
♦ J 10 3 2
♣ 8 7 6 5

Did you wiggle your toes automatically when you saw this hand? You have 10 high card points. Partner has at least 16 points to qualify for an opening bid of 1NT. Partner could have as many as 18 points. The conclusion is that your side has between 26 and 28 total points. This is enough to go for one of the game bonuses.

Focus on 3NT, 4♥, and 4♠. You want to play in the major suit if you have an eight-card or longer trump fit. Otherwise, you want to play in 3NT. With this hand, it doesn't appear that there's a fit in a major suit, so you should choose 3NT. You do this by jumping directly to 3NT as responder. You have all the information you need to make the decision. As captain, you can place the contract for the partnership. Here are some more examples:

♠ K 9 3
♥ Q J 9 7 6 5
♦ A 10
♣ 3 2

Toe wiggling time again. There are 10 high card points plus two points for the six-card heart suit. The partnership has at least 26 combined points, even if partner has the minimum end of the range for an opening 1NT bid. You want to go for the game bonus. The game contract to choose this time is with hearts as the trump suit. Partner's balanced hand contains at least two hearts, and you have six. The total is eight—enough to recommend it as the trump suit. Jump directly to 4♥.

♠ K 9 3
♥ 3 2
♦ A 10
♣ Q J 9 7 6 5

This hand is similar to the previous example. You have 10 high card points plus 2 points for the six-card suit. The difference is that your fit is in a minor suit, clubs, rather than a major suit. Rather than trying for a game level contract of 5♣, go for the nine-trick contract in notrump. Jump to 3NT. You'll be in good company. The best players in the world like to stay away from those minor suit games.

Asking for More Information

There are times when you'll require a little more information from opener even though the 1NT opening bid is quite specific. If we return to our restaurant analogy, you might say, "That sounds like a nice place to eat, but I want to be sure they serve pasta. Do you know what they have on the menu?" Sometimes, you need to know a little more about partner's strength; sometimes, a little more about partner's distribution.

Suppose partner opens 1NT, showing 16–18 points, and this is your hand:

♠ K Q 8
♥ J 5 4
♦ 9 4 3
♣ K 7 6 5

Notrump looks like a good place to play the contract, but it's not clear whether the partnership should stop in partscore or go to the game level. You have 9 high card points. If partner has only 16 points, then the combined total is 25. That's not quite enough for a game contract. If partner has 17 or 18 points, however, there should be enough combined strength.

You could simply guess, and either pass or go all the way to 3NT, but there's another choice. Respond 2NT, moving toward the game bonus without actually bidding it. This sends partner the message that you're interested in reaching the game level but would like more information. By raising the level to 2NT, rather than passing, you're sending partner an invitation. With only 16 points, you want partner to decline the invitation and pass. With the upper end of the range, 17 or 18 points, you want partner to accept the invitation and continue to 3NT.

Sometimes, you're sure there's enough combined strength for a game bonus, but you aren't sure whether to play in a trump suit or in notrump. You need to know more about partner's distribution. Suppose you have this hand:

♠ A J 9 7 5
♥ 9 2
♦ A J 3
♣ 10 5 4

You have 10 high card points plus 1 point for the fifth spade—a total of 11 points. You want to take the partnership to a game level contract, but it's not clear whether to choose 3NT or 4♠. If partner has three or more spades, the partnership has an eight-card major suit fit and belongs in 4♠. If partner has only two spades, there's no major suit fit, and the partnership belongs in a game contract of 3NT.

You could make your best guess and jump to 3NT or 4♠, but there's a way to get more information from partner. Jump to 3♠. This response asks opener to bid 4♠ with three or more spades but to bid 3NT with only two spades. This will get you to the best contract.

This brings up an interesting point. Some of your responses have ended the bidding conversation. Others have invited or insisted that opener bid again. How does opener know whether or not to bid again? This is a good time to introduce you to the bidding messages.

The Three Bidding Messages

Every bid you make carries a message. The bidding conversation is like other conversations. You have expectations. For example, when you say "Goodbye," you don't expect any further conversation. If you ask, "Do you want to leave at seven o'clock or eight o'clock?" you expect a reply. If you make a general comment such as "What a nice day!" you may or may not get a response. There are similar expectations in a bidding conversation.

Sign-off Bids

$$\overset{O}{1NT} \to \overset{R}{2S} \quad \overset{O}{Pass}$$

When partner opens 1NT and you respond 2♠, you're sending a signal for opener to pass. As the captain, you've decided that the best contract for the partnership is a partscore with spades as the trump suit. This is called a *sign-off bid*. In response to an opening bid of 1NT, the bid of any suit at the two level is a sign-off bid, asking opener to pass.*

Learning the expectations that go along with each bid is part of the language of bidding. The more you know about the messages you're sending and receiving, the better your bidding will become. Both partners need to know what to expect.

There are different styles of bidding that can be used by each partnership. Throughout this book, we'll stick with the most common interpretation of each bidding message.

On those toe wiggling hands with 10 or more points, you took the partnership right to the game bonus level of 3NT, 4♥, or 4♠ when you had enough information to make the decision. These are also sign-off bids. It's expected partner will pass. It's like saying goodbye.

In the bidding conversation, most sign-off bids occur after one partner has limited the hand to a narrow range of strength and distribution. The other partner can then take on the role of captain and place the contract.

---

*A response of 2♣ is often reserved for a special purpose, but it's beyond the scope of this book and is covered in the second book in this series, *Better Bridge—Bidding*.

Invitational Bids

When opener started with 1NT and you responded 2NT, you expected partner to either pass or to bid 3NT. You were sending an *invitational* message.

The 1NT opening bid is another example of a bid that carries an invitational message. Responder can pass or bid on, depending on the nature of the hand.

2 NT = invitational

Forcing Bids

Bids that require partner to bid again are called *forcing* bids. They're like a specific question that requires a response—"Do you want to leave at 7 o'clock or 8 o'clock?" A response of 3♥ or 3♠ to an opening bid of 1NT carries a forcing message. Opener is being asked a specific question—"Do you want to be in 3NT or game in the major suit, 4♥ or 4♠?" Opener isn't expected to pass.

Knowing which bids are forcing during the auction is very important. Partner is expecting you to keep bidding and will be disappointed if you drop the conversation in mid-air. We'll hear a lot more about forcing bids in the next chapter.

Dorothy Hayden Truscott, one of the best players in the world, has this to say about the bidding messages:

> "It's hard to overemphasize the importance of forcing bids. They're as vital to bridge players as traffic lights are to drivers of motor vehicles. The different kinds of forcing and non-forcing bids are the traffic signals of the partnership. If one partner is ignorant of their meaning, chaos will often follow, and attempted manslaughter shouldn't be ruled out."

Now, personally, I like playing with partners who consider all my bids interesting—although I'd like to avoid running red lights.

Summary

After the opening bid of 1NT, responder has a lot of information about the combined strength and distribution of the hands. Responder knows that opener has 16, 17, or 18 points and a balanced hand. By adding up the points in the combined hands, responder can decide whether the partnership should stop in partscore or try for the game bonus. Knowing that opener has at least two or three cards in every suit, responder can usually determine if there's a suitable trump suit.

This puts responder in the role of captain, conducting the partnership to the best contract. Responder can use the following guidelines:

0–7 points	Bid two of a suit with a five-card or longer suit, asking opener to pass. Otherwise, pass.
8–9 points	Bid 2NT, inviting opener to carry on to game.
10 or more points	Bid 4♥ or 4♠ with a six-card suit. Bid 3♥ or 3♠ with a five-card suit, asking opener to choose between 3NT and 4♥ or 4♠. Otherwise, bid 3NT.

Each bid that a player makes sends one of three messages. It can be a sign-off bid, asking partner to stop. It can be an invitational bid, leaving the final decision to partner. It can be a forcing bid, asking partner to bid again.

The 1NT opener has to recognize responder's bidding message. When responder bids a suit at the two level or bids to the game level, opener is expected to pass. If responder bids 2NT, opener is being invited to bid again. If responder jumps to the three level in a suit, opener is expected to bid again.

Exercises

1. What range of strength does opener show by starting the bidding with 1NT? *16~18 pts*

2. Which player has the role of captain after a 1NT opening bid? *responder*

3. What are the three game bonus levels that are most frequently considered by the captain? *3 NT, 4H, 4S*

4. How many combined points are required for a reasonable chance to make a game level contract? *26*

5. How many points does responder need to take the partnership right to the game level after an opening bid of 1NT? *10*

6. What kind of hand would responder have to bid a suit at the two level after an opening bid of 1NT? *0~7 5 card or longer*

7. What are the three types of bidding message? *sign off, invitational, forcing*

8. What message is sent by a response of 4♥ to an opening bid of 1NT? *16~18 sign-off ... 4 card Hs*

9. What is an invitational bid that responder can make after an opening bid of 1NT? *2 NT*

10. What would you respond with each of the following hands after partner has opened the bidding with 1NT?

Pass 6

a) ♠ 8 4
♥ Q 9 6 5
♦ J 10 6 4
♣ K 5 4

b) ♠ A 9 8
♥ K 7 5
♦ Q 9 5
♣ Q 10 9 6
11 3NT

c) ♠ 8 4 *4*
♥ 2
♦ Q 10 8 6 5 3 *2D*
♣ 10 7 4 2

10 4S

d) ♠ A J 8 7 4 3
♥ K 6
♦ 6 4
♣ 9 7 3

e) ♠ J 9 8
♥ 7 5 3
♦ K Q 9 5
♣ Q J 7
9 2NT

f) ♠ K J 8
♥ 10 7 3
♦ 6 4
♣ A Q 10 6 4
3NT 11

Answers to Exercises

1. **16, 17, or 18 points.**

2. **Responder**. The partner of the 1NT opener knows most about the combined hands.

3. **3NT, 4 ♥, and 4♠**. The captain rarely considers 5♣ or 5 ♦.

4. **26**. With fewer than 26 points, the partnership should stop in partscore.

5. **10**. Wiggle those toes.

6. **0–7 points and a five-card or longer suit.**

7. **Sign-off, invitational, and forcing**.

8. **4 ♥** is a sign-off bid, asking opener to pass.

9. **2NT**. This is an invitational response showing 8 or 9 points. Opener can pass with only 16 points or carry on to game with 17 or 18 points.

10a) **Pass**. With 0–7 points and no five-card or longer suit, leave the partnership in a partscore of 1NT.

10b) **3NT**. With 10 or more points and no major suit fit, take the partnership to the 3NT game bonus level.

10c) **2 ♦**. This is a sign-off bid telling partner that you want to play in a partscore with diamonds as the trump suit.

10d) **4♠**. You have 8 high card points plus 2 points for the six-card suit. With 10 points, wiggle your toes, and jump to game in the major suit. Opener has at least two spades, so there's an eight-card or longer fit.

10e) **2NT**. The raise to 2NT shows 8–9 points and invites opener to continue if holding the upper range of strength.

10f) **3NT**. With 10 high card points plus 1 for the five-card suit, there's enough combined strength for game. Even if there's a minor suit fit, 3NT should be easier to make than 5♣.

♣ ◆ ♥ ♠ ♣ ◆ ♥ ♠ ♣ ◆ ♥ ♠ **7** ♣ ◆ ♥ ♠ ♣ ◆ ♥ ♠ ◆ ♥ ♠ ♣

Responding—
A Second Look

"Beginning of the teaching for life,
The instruction for well-being . . .
Knowing how to answer one who speaks,
To reply to one who sends a message."

—AMENEMOPE,
[11th century B.C.]

Sometimes, conversations are very specific—"I'd like to eat at Winston's tonight, and if we get there by 5:30, we'll have time to get to our 7 o'clock class." An opening bid of 1NT is very specific. It limits the hand to a narrow range of points and a balanced hand pattern. This helps responder decide on the best contract for the partnership with little or no further information from opener.

Some conversations aren't that exact—"Let's go out for dinner tonight. Any suggestions?" An opening bid of 1♥ is not too specific. Opener can have anywhere from 13 to 21 points, and might have a balanced hand or a very unbalanced hand pattern.

As responder, you still have your eye on reaching the best contract for the partnership, but you usually can't make the decision in only one bid. You don't have enough information. The bidding conversation is likely to go on a little longer before the partnership can settle on the best spot.

Responding to One-of-a-Suit

When partner starts with one-of-a-suit, there are four possibilities: 1♣, 1♦, 1♥, or 1♠. Partner is suggesting a trump suit and showing a hand worth somewhere between 13 and 21 points. This is only the first bid in the conversation, and opener is inviting you to respond.

There's a difference in the structure of the conversation after a suit bid as compared to the conversation following an opening notrump bid. Notrump opening bids are limited to a narrow three-point range. As responder, you often know enough to place the contract in one bid. This is a sign-off bid. You can respond on very few points when you have a sign-off bid available because opener is now expected to pass.

After an opening bid of one-in-a-suit, there's no sign-off bid available to responder other than pass. The reason for this is that opener could have as few as 13 or as many as 21 points. Opener's hand could be balanced or unbalanced. Responder doesn't have enough information to insist that opener accept a final decision after one response. Let's take a look at each of responder's options.

Passing

Responder doesn't have to continue the conversation after an opening bid of one-of-a-suit. The partnership may already be high enough. This is usually the case when responder has a hand worth about 0–5 points.

Opener could have as few as 13 points. When responder holds only 2 or 3 points, the partnership is probably already too high. The other partnership holds the majority of strength and should probably be bidding for the contract. You certainly don't want to get any higher. Even if opener is near the upper end of the range of strength for an opening bid at the one level, there's not enough combined strength for the partnership to reach the game level. The partnership should stop in partscore. When opener starts the bidding with one-of-a-suit, the general guideline for responder is:

- Pass with 0–5 points.

For example, partner opens the bidding 1♥, and this is your hand:

♠ 7 5 2
♥ 9 3
♦ Q J 8 7 5
♣ 10 8 3

Pass. 1♥ may not be the best contract for your side, but you can't afford to get the partnership any higher while searching for a better spot.

When you hold about 6 or more points, you should keep the auction going in case opener's strength is close to the upper end of the range, and the partnership belongs at the game level. Let's look at the choices you have.

Agreeing with Partner

One of the objectives of the auction is for the partnership to agree on a suitable trump suit. If you like the suit that opener is suggesting, you can show your agreement by *supporting*, or *raising*, partner's suit. For example, the auction might start off in this manner:

WEST	NORTH	EAST	SOUTH
	1♥	Pass	2♥

North has suggested hearts as the trump suit, and South has agreed by raising the suggested trump suit to the two level. The partnership has settled on a suitable trump suit through the auction. The only remaining decision will be whether to stop in a partscore contract or try for the game bonus. We'll get to that later.

Some partnerships prefer to have a five-card or longer suit when they open the bidding in a major suit, 1♥ or 1♠. If that's the case, responder needs only three cards to support the suit. In other partnerships, opener could have four cards in the suit to open the bidding 1♥ or 1♠. You'd need four cards in the suit if the partnership is to have an eight-card fit. The exact number of cards you need depends a little on the partnership style. We'll put such variations aside for now, and you can use the following guideline:

- To show support for opener's suit, you should have at least three cards in the suit and, preferably, four or more cards.

For example, consider these three hands you might hold when partner opens the bidding 1♥:

1)	♠ J 8	2)	♠ J 8	3)	♠ J 9 8
	♥ 10 9 7 3		♥ Q 10 9		♥ Q 10
	♦ A 9 6 4		♦ A 9 6 4		♦ A 9 6 4
	♣ Q 8 2		♣ 8 7 3 2		♣ 8 7 3 2

With the first hand, you should be happy to show support for partner's suit because you have four trump. The partnership will have at least an eight-card fit. You don't need any high cards in partner's suit to show support. It's the combined length that's important.

You could also support partner's suit with the second hand. Although you would like to have four cards in the suit, three-card support is adequate. With the third hand, however, you shouldn't support partner's suit right away. The likelihood is that you don't have an eight-card or longer fit. Only if partner were to repeat the suit later in the auction—showing some extra length—would you consider agreeing on hearts as the trump suit.

You want to tell partner that you agree on the choice of the trump suit. You also want to provide partner with some information about the strength of your hand. This information will allow the partnership to decide whether or not to go for one of the bonus levels. You send this message through the level to which you raise partner's suit as follows:

Raising Opener's Suit

0–5 points	Pass.
6–10 points	Raise to the two level.
11–12 points	Raise to the three level.
13 or more points	Raise to the game level.

This is a straightforward approach: the more strength you have, the more you bid. There are other methods that can be used to show various ranges of strength, but they're beyond the scope of this book. The style used here is sometimes known as *limit raises*, since each raise is limited to a specific range of strength. Let's see how it works with each of the following hands after partner has opened the bidding 1♥.

♠ 10 7 5   *6-10*
♥ Q 8 4 2
♦ A 7 3   *7 pts*
♣ J 9 6
     2/t

You have support for partner's suit, and 7 high card points. It would be pleasant to pass, and let partner try to take seven tricks with hearts as trump, but you can't be sure that the partnership doesn't have the combined strength to hit the ball over the fence and get the game bonus. Partner's opening bid shows between 13 and 21 points. If partner has 19, 20, or 21 points—the upper range for an opening bid at the one level—the partnership should be going for the game bonus. You show the support for partner's suit while moving toward the game level in a very mild manner by responding 2♥. This will give partner a chance to show extra strength on the next bid. If partner doesn't have anything extra, the partnership can rest comfortably at the partscore level.

♠ A 7 5   *3 H*
♥ Q 8 4 2
♦ A 7 3   *11 pt,*
♣ J 9 6
     (11-12

Now the hand is worth 11 points. The partnership belongs at the game level if opener has 15 or more points but should stop short of the game level if opener has only 13 or 14 points. You move toward game a little more vigorously by responding 3♥, raising opener's suit to the three level. That allows the partnership to stop in partscore if opener has no extra strength. With a little bit extra, partner can accept your invitation and bid on to the 4♥ game.

♠ A K 5   *H H*
♥ Q 8 4 2
♦ A 7 3   *14*
♣ J 9 6

This time you have 14 points. Since partner's opening bid shows at least 13 points, the partnership has enough combined strength to go for the game bonus. By raising to 4♥, you make sure the partnership reaches the bonus level.

I have to warn you that some players have different opinions about jumping directly to the game level. Experienced players often like to go through more detailed bidding steps on the way to a game level contract. You can read about some of them in the *Better Bridge— Bidding* book, but the method suggested here is straightforward and requires little memory work. You'll still have time left to take the dog for a walk.

You could keep your slam bidding simple, and continue along the same lines—raising to 5♥ with 17 or 18 points to invite opener to bid slam, and going directly to 6♥ with 19 or more points. There are fancier methods for reaching a slam contract, but these are best left for another book.

There's one detail connected to supporting partner's suit that's worth considering at this point. Suppose you pick up this hand:

> ♠ K 9 6 3
> ♥ —
> ♦ Q 9 6 5 2
> ♣ A 8 6 5

[handwritten: 10 pt. 6 - 10 = 2 level]

Partner starts the bidding 1♥. How do you feel about responding to this opening bid? Perhaps your shoulders droop a little. How disappointing. Partner has suggested as trump a suit in which you're void. On the other hand, how would you feel if partner opens the bidding 1♠? You aren't permitted to stand on your chair and say, "Wow!" In fact, good table manners should stop you from making an exclamation even if you're still sitting down. Nevertheless, it's safe to say that you prefer partner's opening bid of 1♠ to an opening bid of 1♥.

There's good reason for this. Suppose that spades are the trump suit, and one of your opponents leads the ♥A. Your lowly ♠3 is more powerful than the ♥A. The void in hearts is valuable when spades are trump. This improvement in the value of your hand when you have support for partner's suit is reflected by assigning points to short suits using the following scale:

[handwritten: responder includes when suit could be supported]

Dummy Points	
Void	5 points
Singleton	3 points
Doubleton	1 points

These are used in place of length points when you're planning to support partner's suit. They're referred to as *dummy points* because your hand will eventually go down on the table as the dummy if you support partner's suit—declarer is the player who first mentioned the suit.

You would start out valuing the above hand as 10 points—9 high card points plus 1 length point for the five-card suit. If partner were to open the bidding 1♥, the hand has not improved in value and would still be worth about 10 points. If partner were to open 1♠, however, you would revalue the hand using dummy points instead of length points because you have support for partner's suit. The hand would now be worth 14 points—9 high card points plus 5 dummy points for the void in hearts.

Revaluing your hand using dummy points will often affect the level to which you raise partner's suit. With the above hand, you now have enough strength to raise partner all the way to the game level, 4♠. If you didn't revalue your hand, you would have responded only 2♠, showing about 6–10 points. Here's another example.

♠ A Q 4 3   *8 + 3*
♥ 4
♦ Q 8 6 5
♣ 10 7 4 3

You would be disappointed if partner opens the bidding 1♥, and you'd continue to value the hand as only 8 high card points. If partner opens with 1♠, you'd feel much more positive about the hand. You've found a suitable trump fit, and the singleton heart should prove useful. The singleton heart is not as valuable as an ace because it won't win the first trick in the suit. It's similar in value to a king because you could win the second trick in the suit if hearts are led by trumping with the ♠3. That's why it's given a value of 3 points when spades are going to be the trump suit. Your hand is now worth 11 points—8 high card points plus 3 dummy points for the singleton. You would raise opener's 1♠ bid to 3♠, showing a hand in the 11–12 point range.

Responding in a New Suit

Your partner may suggest a trump suit, but you may not like the suggestion. As responder, you can make a suggestion of your own.

You don't need any high cards in a suit to suggest it because the partnership is interested in length, not strength, when it comes to the trump suit. Any suit that contains four or more cards can be shown. There are some limitations, however. To bid a new suit at the one level, you should have at least 6 points. If you have to go to the two level to show your suit, you should have at least 11 points.

Responding in a new suit requires some minimum amount of strength because a new suit by responder is a forcing bid. If this were a pop-up book, I'd have something pop out at this point to emphasize the importance of the previous sentence. When responder bids a new suit, opener is expected to bid again. Let's see how this affects the structure of the bidding.

Although you need at least 6 points to respond in a new suit at the one level, there's no upper limit to the strength you can have. Since a new suit is forcing, partner will bid again, and you'll have the opportunity to show your extra strength later in the auction. Consider each of the following hands you might hold as responder after partner starts the bidding 1♦:

♠ K J 8 7 3
♥ 4 3
♦ 10 2
♣ Q 9 6 2

With this hand, you would like to suggest spades as the trump suit, rather than diamonds. You can do this by responding 1♠, bidding a new suit at the one level. You have only 6 high card points plus 1 point for the five-card suit, but you want to keep the auction going in case the partnership has enough combined strength for the game bonus. Opener could have a very strong hand of about 19–21 points. Even if opener doesn't have a strong hand, the partnership would still like to find the best partscore contract.

♠ K J 8 7 3
♥ A Q
♦ 10 2
♣ Q 9 6 2

This hand is worth 13 points—12 HCPs plus 1 for the five-card suit. The partnership must have the 26 combined points needed for a game level contract because opener has at least 13 points. You still respond 1♠, showing your suit. The partnership is searching for the best denomination in which to play the contract. It's too early in the auction to decide whether the contract should be 3NT, 4♠, or something else. You don't have enough information about opener's hand. The 1♠ response is a forcing bid, and opener will bid again, further describing the hand. This gives you more of the information you need to agree on an appropriate game contract.

♠ K J 8 7 3
♥ 4 3
♦ K Q 10 2
♣ Q 9

This hand introduces an important consideration. You do have support for partner's suit but finding a major suit fit takes priority over a minor suit fit. You need only ten tricks for the game bonus in a major suit, whereas you need eleven tricks for the game bonus with a minor suit as trump. As responder, your first priority should be to try to find a major suit fit. If you can't find a major suit fit, then you can go back to the minor suit. Respond 1♠ with this hand. If opener doesn't like spades, you can show support for diamonds at your next opportunity.

♠ K J 8 7 3
♥ A K 4 3
♦ 10 2
♣ 6 2

With this hand you would also respond 1♠. With a choice of suits to show partner, bid the longer suit. You're searching for the longest combined fit, not the strongest.

♠ K J 8 7
♥ A K 4 3
♦ 10 2
♣ 9 6 2

When you have a choice of four-card suits to tell partner about, the guideline is to bid the first one you come to on the one-way street. With this hand, you respond 1♥. That gives the partnership the best chance of finding a fit. If partner likes hearts, you've found a trump fit right away. If partner doesn't like hearts, there's still room at the one level for partner to show a spade suit, and you'll find your fit in that suit.

♠ 8 7 3
♥ A K 4
♦ 10 2
♣ K J 8 7 3

After partner opens the bidding 1♦, you have to go to the two level to show your club suit. You would respond 2♣. You need about 11 or more points to respond in a new suit at the two level. You need the extra strength because the auction is getting higher while you're continuing to search for a suitable trump suit. With this hand, you have 11 high card points plus 1 for the five-card suit, so it's safe to move up a level even though you don't yet know exactly where the partnership is headed.

Responding in Notrump

Suppose partner opens the bidding 1♦, and you hold this hand:

♠ Q 9 3
♥ K 8 4
♦ 4 2
♣ K 10 9 7 4

You have 8 high card points plus 1 for the five-card club suit, giving you a total of 9 points. You don't have support for partner's diamond suit and don't have a suit you can show at the one level. You would have to go to the two level to tell partner about the club suit—but that requires 11 or more points. You have too much to say pass; you would miss out on the game bonus if partner has a strong hand of about 17 or more points. What's left?

A response of 1NT is used when you have a hand of about 6–10 points, and nothing else to bid. It keeps the auction going while saying that you can't support partner's suit and don't have a suit to show at the one level.

My students often tell me it's unsettling that a bid of 1NT shows a balanced hand of 16–18 points when used by the opening bidder, but it has a different meaning when used by responder. Many games have rules for the opening move or play that don't apply when the game is in progress. In tennis, for example, the serve is made within a very narrow boundary. Once the ball is in play, the boundary widens.

The serve—or opening 1NT bid—has specific requirements. Once the ball is in play, the bid takes on a different meaning. A 1NT bid by responder shows a hand with 6–10 points. It doesn't require any particular shape, as can be seen by looking at a more extreme example:

♠ Q 9
♥ K 8 4
♦ 4
♣ J 10 8 7 4 3 2

If partner opens 1♦, you should respond 1NT with this hand. You have only 9 points—6 high card points plus 3 points for the seven-card suit. That's not enough to move to the two level in a new suit. Most players new to the game are a little uncomfortable with this, but the 1NT response is useful in terms of partnership economy. If you respond 2♣ on the above hand, you may find that you've spent more than you can afford, and the partnership could end up in a contract that can't be made.

The meaning of other notrump responses, such as 2NT and 3NT, goes beyond the scope of this book, since there are different partnership styles. A simple approach is to use a response of 2NT to show a balanced hand of 11–12 points, and 3NT to show a balanced hand of 13–15 points. You don't need to use these responses, however. Once you have 11 or more points, you have enough strength to show your own suit, whether it's at the one level or the two level.

Responding to Other Opening Bids

Most of the time, opener starts the bidding at the one level, but there are times when the auction starts at the two level or higher.

Responding to Two-of-a-Suit

Opener starts the bidding at the two level with a hand of about 22 or more points. The most important thing to remember when responding to an opening bid of two-in-a-suit is that it's a forcing bid. Partner wants to be in at least a game level contract and is probably wondering if a slam level contract is possible. You're expected to bid, even if you have little or no strength.

Suppose you have a hand that falls into the 0–5 point range. You would pass with such a weak hand if partner opened the bidding at the one level since there's no real likelihood of getting to a game level contract. You can't pass, however, when opener starts with a suit at the two level because there should be enough combined strength for the game bonus level even though you don't have much. In this situation, respond 2NT to send the message to partner that you have fewer than 6 points. That keeps the auction going and warns partner not to get too excited about the prospect of going beyond the game level.

If you have more than 5 points, do what comes naturally. You can show support for partner's suit by raising it to the three level, or you can bid a suit of your own.

Let's see how all this works when your partner starts the bidding 2♥, and you hold each of the following hands.

♠ 3 2
♥ J 9 4 3
♦ Q 10 6 5
♣ A 8 2

You have support for partner's suggested trump suit and can show this by raising to 3♥. Now that the trump suit has been selected, the partnership can decide whether to stop at the game level or try for the slam bonus. That will depend on exactly how strong a hand partner holds.

♠ 9 3 2
♥ 4 3
♦ Q 10 6 5
♣ J 9 8 2

With only 3 points, you'd like to pass with this hand. Remember, however, that partner is insisting that you bid—partner's "treat," so to speak. You have to say something to keep the auction going. This is where you respond 2NT. This is often referred to as a *negative response* because it sends the message that you have a very weak hand and are bidding only because partner has made a forcing bid.

Responding to Two Notrump

The opening bid of 2NT is a little different. It shows specifically a balanced hand of 22–24 points. Since 2NT is limited to at most 24 points, responder could pass when there isn't enough combined strength for a game level contract. This would be quite rare, since responder needs only about 2 or 3 points to be reasonably confident that the partnership has the combined 26 points for a game contract.

Responding to 2NT is similar to responding to an opening bid of 1NT. After the opening 2NT bid, responder usually knows enough about the combined strength and distribution to decide on the contract in one bid. Let's look at a couple of examples.

open 2NT = 22 pts (handwritten)

♠ 3 2 *5*
♥ J 4 3
♦ Q 10 9 4
♣ Q 8 6 3

You have 5 points, and partner has at least 22. Take the partnership to the game level by responding 3NT. There's no need to look for a minor suit trump fit. Even if you found one, it's easier to take nine tricks in a notrump contract than eleven tricks with a minor suit as trump.

♠ 10 4
♥ Q 9 7 5 4 3
♦ 8 6   *4*
♣ 8 5 2

Respond 4♥. Partner's opening 2NT shows a balanced hand with at least two hearts. You have an eight-card major suit fit. Partner's hand has enough strength to put this ten-trick game within reach. You have 2 high card points plus 2 points for the length in the heart suit. Your total of 4 points added to partner's 22 or more points gives the partnership at least 26 combined points.

Responding to Three-of-a-Suit — *Preemptive* — 3♥ (handwritten: *seven card suit*)

An opening bid at the three level is called a *preemptive bid* showing a good seven-card or longer suit with less than the values for an opening bid at the one level. For an opening bid of 3♥, partner's hand might look something like this:

9 (handwritten)

♠ 2
♥ K Q J 9 7 4 3
♦ 10 8 5
♣ 7 4

As responder, you should usually pass. It's unlikely there's a better choice of trump suit, and the partnership is probably already high enough—perhaps too high. Respond only if you think there's a good possibility of making a game level contract. Since partner will have 10 or fewer points, you need 16 or more points to go for the game bonus. Consider these examples after partner starts the auction with a preemptive bid of 3♥:

♠ K Q 7 4
♥ 2
♦ A J 9
♣ Q J 10 5 2

Pass. You have 14 points—13 high card points plus 1 for the five-card suit. Had partner started the bidding 1♥, you would be thinking of reaching a suitable game level contract. Partner, however, has announced a hand with a very long heart suit, and limited strength. Even though you don't like partner's choice of trump suit, partner's hand will be able to take tricks only if hearts are the trump suit. It's unlikely there's enough combined strength for a game bonus, so you should pass and wish partner luck when you put your hand down as the dummy.

♠ K 10 6 4
♥ A 10 2
♦ 4
♣ A Q J 6 2

Respond 4♥. With this hand, you have support for partner's suit and can value your hand using dummy points. You have 14 high card points plus 3 for the singleton diamond, giving you a total of 17. That should be enough to go for the game bonus even if partner's hand is worth only 9 or 10 points.

A more complete discussion of the tactics associated with preemptive bids is contained in *Better Bridge—Bidding*. For now, keep in mind that opener is showing a weak hand with a long suit, and you won't have much trouble deciding what to do.

Summary

An opening bid of 1♣, 1♦, 1♥, or 1♠ is an invitational bid showing a hand of about 13–21 points. As the responder to the opening bid, you have the following choices:

- Pass. You do this with a hand of about 0–5 points.
- Support partner's suit. You do this by raising to the two level with 6–10 points, the three level with 11–12 points, and the game level with 13 or more points. Use dummy points to value the hand—5 for a void, 3 for a singleton, 1 for a doubleton—and remember that finding a major suit fit takes priority over supporting opener's minor suit.
- Bid a new suit. You need 6 or more points to bid a new suit at the one level and 11 or more points if you have to go to the two level. A bid of a new suit by responder is a forcing bid, and opener is expected to bid again.
- Bid 1NT. This shows 6–10 points when you can't support partner's suit or suggest a new suit at the one level.

An opening bid of 2♣, 2♦, 2♥, or 2♠ is a forcing bid showing a hand of 22 or more points. Responder must keep the auction going by supporting partner's suit, bidding a new suit, or using the negative response of 2NT to show a weak hand of 0–5 points.

An opening bid of 2NT is an invitational bid showing a balanced hand of 22–24 points. Responder should put the partnership in the best game level contract with 3 or more points.

An opening bid of 3♣, 3♦, 3♥, or 3♠ is an invitational bid showing a long suit with less than the values for an opening bid. Responder should usually pass with fewer than 16 points; otherwise, take the partnership to the game level.

[handwritten notes:]

Opener
1 level – 13–21 pts

Opener
2C 2D 2H 2S =
22 or more pts

Resp. 2 level – 6–10
3 level – 11–12 pts
game level – 13 or more – use dummy
INT – 6–10 pts

Resp.
2NT – 0–5 pts

5–3–1

Exercises

1. Partner opens the bidding 1♣. What would you respond with each of the following hands?

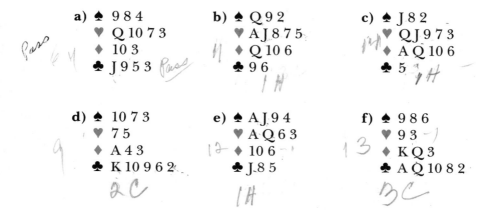

a) ♠ 9 8 4
  ♥ Q 10 7 3
  ♦ 10 3
  ♣ J 9 5 3

b) ♠ Q 9 2
  ♥ A J 8 7 5
  ♦ Q 10 6
  ♣ 9 6

c) ♠ J 8 2
  ♥ Q J 9 7 3
  ♦ A Q 10 6
  ♣ 5

d) ♠ 10 7 3
  ♥ 7 5
  ♦ A 4 3
  ♣ K 10 9 6 2

e) ♠ A J 9 4
  ♥ A Q 6 3
  ♦ 10 6
  ♣ J 8 5

f) ♠ 9 8 6
  ♥ 9 3
  ♦ K Q 3
  ♣ A Q 10 8 2

2. Partner opens the bidding 1♠. What would you respond with each of the following hands?

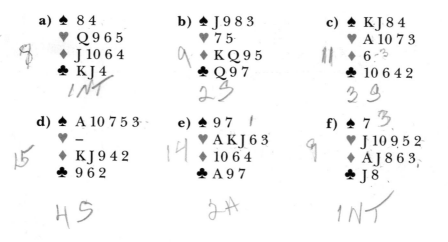

a) ♠ 8 4
  ♥ Q 9 6 5
  ♦ J 10 6 4
  ♣ K J 4

b) ♠ J 9 8 3
  ♥ 7 5
  ♦ K Q 9 5
  ♣ Q 9 7

c) ♠ K J 8 4
  ♥ A 10 7 3
  ♦ 6
  ♣ 10 6 4 2

d) ♠ A 10 7 5 3
  ♥ –
  ♦ K J 9 4 2
  ♣ 9 6 2

e) ♠ 9 7
  ♥ A K J 6 3
  ♦ 10 6 4
  ♣ A 9 7

f) ♠ 7
  ♥ J 10 9 5 2
  ♦ A J 8 6 3
  ♣ J 8

3. Partner opens the bidding 2♦ What would you respond with each of the following hands?

a) ♠ Q 8 4
   ♥ QJ 4
   ♦ K 7 6 3
   ♣ 10 7 4

   3D

b) ♠ AJ 8 6 3
   ♥ 7 5
   ♦ 9 4
   ♣ Q 10 8 7

   2S

c) ♠ J 8 4
   ♥ 10 7 3
   ♦ 9 6
   ♣ J 10 7 5 3

   2NT

4. Partner opens the bidding 3♠. What would you respond with each of the following hands?

a) ♠ 6
   ♥ QJ 8 5 2
   ♦ K Q 7 6 3
   ♣ 7 4

   Pass

b) ♠ 6 3
   ♥ KJ 7 3
   ♦ A Q J 4
   ♣ Q 8 7

   Pass

c) ♠ K 9 4
   ♥ 7 3
   ♦ A K J 6 4
   ♣ K Q 5

   4S

Answers to Exercises

1a) Pass. With only 3 points, you don't have enough to bid.

1b) 1♥. With 9 high card points plus 1 for the five-card suit, keep the auction going by suggesting a new suit.

1c) 1♥. With a choice of suits, show the longest suit first.

1d) 2♣. With support for partner's suit, and a hand in the 6–10 point range, raise to the two level.

1e) 1♥. With a choice of four-card suits to show, start with the lower-ranking to leave the most room to find a fit.

1f) 3♣. There are 11 high card points plus 1 for the five-card suit. A jump raise to the three level shows support for opener's suit, and about 11–12 points.

2a) 1NT. With 7 points you want to keep the auction going, but don't have enough strength to bid a new suit at the two level. Use the response of 1NT.

2b) 2♠. A raise to the two level shows support for partner's suit, and about 6–10 points.

2c) 3♠. With support for partner's suit, value the hand using dummy points. You have 8 high card points plus 3 points for the singleton diamond. A raise to the three level shows 11–12 points.

2d) 4♠. With support for partner's suit, this hand is worth 8 HCPs plus 5 dummy points for the void in hearts. With 13 points opposite partner's 13 or more points for the opening bid, take the partnership to the game level.

2e) 2♥. You have 12 high card points plus 1 for the five-card suit. That's more than enough to bid a new suit at the two level.

2f) 1NT. You have 9 points—7 high card points plus 1 point for each of the five-card suits. Although the hand is not balanced, you don't have the required 11 points to respond in a new suit at the two level. Instead, use the response of 1NT to show 6–10 points.

3a) 3♦. Show your support for opener's suit by raising to the next level.

3b) 2♠. Without support for partner's suit, bid a suit of your own.

3c) **2NT**. Although you have only 3 points—2 high card points plus 1 for the five-card suit—you can't pass partner's forcing bid. Instead, make use of the negative response of 2NT, telling partner you have a weak hand.

4a) **Pass**. Although you don't like partner's choice of suit, you can't afford to go any higher looking for a better contract.

4b) **Pass**. Partner's preemptive opening bid shows fewer than 13 points. Holding only 13 points, there won't be enough combined strength for a game level contract.

4c) **4♠**. This hand is worth 17 points, so it should be strong enough to undertake a game level contract even if partner has only 9 or 10 points.

Opener Continues the Conversation

"Painting is only a bridge linking the painter's mind with that of the viewer."

— EUGÈNE DELACROIX,
Journal [1893-1895]

The first bid that opener makes starts off a bidding conversation, so opener shouldn't be surprised to be bidding again, or *rebidding*. Conversations rarely end after a single remark. Your partner, the responder, will make a bid, and you need to interpret what's expected of you. In other words, what's the bidding message? There's one message that responder can't give after an opening bid of one-of-a-suit and that's a sign-off message. Responder doesn't know enough about your hand after an opening bid of one-in-a-suit to make a quick decision on the contract. So, responder's bid is either invitational or forcing.

You could have as few as 13 or as many as 21 points, and either a balanced or very unbalanced hand. You need to paint a clearer picture with your rebid. Partner is either inviting you to bid again or asking you to bid again and tell more about your hand.

On your second bid—*opener's rebid*—you want to pick a bid that describes both the strength and the shape of the hand in more detail. To help choose your rebid, start out by placing your hand into one of three ranges of strength.

Small, Medium, or Large

Think of the strength of your hand in terms of small, medium or large. I sometimes use the analogy of the Three Bears when talking to students about opener's rebids. I categorize the points in opener's hand as small, medium, or large and put them in the bears' porridge bowls. A Baby Bear, or minimum, hand is one containing about 13 to 16 points; a Mama Bear, or medium, hand is one worth about 17 or 18 points; a Papa Bear, or maximum, hand is one with 19 to 21 points. Like this:

Minimum Hand   *Medium Hand*   *Maximum Hand*
13 14 15 16   17 18   19 20 21

You can probably come up with a way of remembering the three strength categories without resorting to fairy tales, but it's the principle that's important when trying to choose a suitable rebid. Any hand you've opened at the one level in a suit will fall into one of the three ranges. You open the bidding at the two level with a hand stronger than 21 points. For example, compare these three hands, all of which have the same distribution:

1) ♠ 8 2
    ♥ A Q J 10 9 7
    ♦ A J 3
    ♣ 10 4

2) ♠ 8 2
    ♥ A Q J 10 9 7
    ♦ A K J
    ♣ 10 4

3) ♠ 8 2
    ♥ A Q J 10 9 7
    ♦ A K J
    ♣ K 4

The first hand contains 12 high card points plus 2 points for the six-card suit—a total of 14 points. That's a minimum—or Baby Bear—hand. The second hand contains an additional king, making it worth 17 points. Now it's a medium—Mama Bear—strength hand. The last hand has another king to bring it up to 20 points—a Papa Bear hand. I promise not to mention the bears again.

You would open each of these hands 1♥. When it comes time to make your second bid—your *rebid*—you want to describe your hand so that partner knows whether it falls into the small, medium, or large category. Let's see how you can do this.

After Responder Makes a Forcing Bid

When you open the bidding at the one level in a suit and your partner responds in another suit, partner's response is a forcing bid. Partner could have as few as 6 points to bid a new suit at the one level but could also have 13 or more—enough for the partnership to belong at the game level. So, you shouldn't pass. Partner is expecting to hear more about your hand before the partnership can settle on a suitable contract.

When partner responds in a new suit, you have a number of choices:

- You can tell partner that you like the new suit by supporting, or raising, partner's suit. Once you've agreed on a suit, the partnership has to decide whether or not to go for one of the bonus levels.

- You can suggest another suit if you don't like the suit partner has shown. Partner can then decide between the various possible trump suits or can choose notrump if there's no suitable fit.

- You can suggest playing the contract in notrump, if you have a balanced hand. Partner can then decide whether the contract should be played in a trump suit or notrump.

- You can bid your suit again if you don't have a balanced hand and don't have another suit to suggest. Rebidding your suit gives partner the message that you would really like your suit to be trump.

After deciding on the best choice, you make your rebid at a level that reflects the strength of your hand. With a minimum hand, you rebid as inexpensively as you can. With a medium-strength hand, you can be a bit more aggressive. With a maximum-strength hand, you want to make sure the partnership gets to at least a game bonus level.

Let's see how this works. Suppose you're dealer with this hand:

♠ J 7 6 4
♥ A 4
♦ A K J 4 2
♣ 9 5

You have 13 high card points plus 1 point for the five-card diamond suit, so you open the bidding 1♦. Partner responds 1♠. Since partner will have at least four spades to mention the suit, you're happy to agree on spades as the trump suit. You send partner this message by raising partner's suit. Because your hand falls in the minimum-strength category, you bid 2♠, the most inexpensive bid you can make that tells partner you like spades.

Having found a suitable trump fit, you might wonder why you don't simply pass, leaving the partnership in a contract of 1♠. Remember that you're not expected to pass when responder bids a new suit. Although you have a minimum-strength hand, responder could have 13 or more points. The partnership would have enough to belong at the game bonus level. By raising partner to the next level, you're keeping the auction going, telling partner you like spades as the trump suit and showing a hand in the minimum range, 13–16 points. Responder will now be in a position to decide whether the partnership should stop in partscore or go for the game bonus.

One small point before moving on. In the last chapter, we talked about using dummy points to revalue a hand when planning to support partner's suit. These are 5 points for a void, 3 points for a singleton, and 1 point for a doubleton—instead of length points. This applies to opener as well as responder. Since you're planning to support partner's spade suit with the above hand, you should count 1 point for each of the doubletons, rather than giving yourself an extra point for the five-card diamond suit. That makes the hand worth 15 points instead of 14 points. It still falls in the minimum range, so you'd rebid only 2♠. Suppose, however, the auction starts the same way: you open the bidding 1♦, and partner responds 1♠. You hold this hand:

♠ A 7 6 4
♥ A 4
♦ A K J 4 2
♣ 9 5

There are 16 high card points, but you can add 1 point for each doubleton, since you plan to show support for partner's spade suit. That gives you 18 points, putting the hand in the medium-strength category. With a medium-strength hand, you can be more aggressive with your rebid. Instead of rebidding 2♠ with this hand, you would bid 3♠—jumping a level to show the extra strength. This lets partner know that you like spades and have a hand of about 17 or 18 points. Partner can now decide whether or not to carry on to the game level.

Now, suppose you pick up this hand. The auction starts the same way: you open the bidding 1♦, and partner responds 1♠.

♠ A 7 6 4
♥ A 4
♦ A K J 10 4 2
♣ 9

With support for partner's suit, you can revalue the strength of your hand using dummy points. You count 1 point for the doubleton heart, and 3 points for the singleton club. Together with your 16 high card points, the hand is now worth 20 points.

This is a wonderful hand, and you want to describe the maximum strength while letting partner know that you like spades as the trump suit. You can do this with your rebid by jumping all the way to 4♠.

You can see how the rebids start to fall into a pattern, depending on the strength of opener's hand. With a small hand, opener raises to the next level; with a medium hand, opener jumps a level; with a large hand, opener jumps all the way to the game level.

Let's look at some of the other rebids that opener can make—keeping in mind the principle that the more you have the more you bid. In each of the following examples, you're North, and the auction has started off this way:

WEST	NORTH	EAST	SOUTH
	(YOU)		(PARTNER)
	1♦	Pass	1♥
Pass	?		

♠ A Q 4 3
♥ 7
♦ A Q J 9 3
♣ 10 5 2

You don't like partner's suggestion about the heart suit, but you can offer another choice, spades. With a minimum-strength hand, you show the spade suit at the cheapest available level by rebidding 1♠.

Conversations that start with each partner showing one or two suits might go on for some time until an agreement is reached. Here's another example of giving responder a second choice.

♠ 4 3
♥ 7
♦ A Q J 9 3
♣ K Q 10 5 2

You start by bidding 1♦, the higher-ranking of the two five-card suits. When responder bids 1♥, you can show your second suit by rebidding 2♣. You have to go to the two level to show the club suit.

♠ A 4 3
♥ 7 2
♦ A Q J 9 3
♣ Q 10 5

With this hand, you don't have a second suit to show. Your hand is balanced, however, and you can show this by making your rebid in notrump. With 13 high card points plus 1 point for the five-card suit, you have a minimum-strength hand of 14 points. You would rebid 1NT, bidding at the cheapest available level.

♠ A 4 3
♥ 7 2
♦ A Q J 9
♣ Q 10 5 2

Here you have a choice of showing your other suit, clubs, or telling partner that you have a balanced hand. A rebid of 1NT is a better choice than 2♣ because it keeps the partnership at the one level and also sends responder an accurate picture of the shape your hand.

♠ 4 3
♥ 7
♦ A Q J 9 8 3 2
♣ A 10 5

With 11 high card points plus 3 points for the seven-card suit, your hand falls into the minimum-strength category. You don't like partner's heart suit but have no other suit to suggest, and your hand is not suitable for suggesting a notrump contract. Rebid 2♦, telling partner that you would really like diamonds as the trump suit.

♠ 4 3
♥ 7
♦ A Q J 9 8 3 2
♣ A K 5

This hand is similar to the previous one except that the extra king gives you 17 points, a medium-strength hand. Rebid 3♦, rather than 2♦. Partner will get the message that you have more than minimum strength, since you jumped a level of bidding.

After Responder Makes an Invitational Bid

You have probably been in a situation where you're invited somewhere, and you can either accept or decline the invitation. It's not a command performance. There are two bids responder can make that are invitational. After these responses, you, as the opener, can either bid again or pass. Think of it as an invitation to consider the game bonus. That's what this game is all about.

Responder Raises Your Suit

The first invitational bid by responder occurs when responder supports the suit that you suggested with your opening bid. For example:

WEST	NORTH	EAST	SOUTH
	(YOU)		(PARTNER)
	1♥	Pass	2♥
Pass	?		

The partnership has found a suitable trump suit, but that's not necessarily the end of the conversation. Remember, responder knows only that you have somewhere between 13 and 21 points. You need to be more specific when it comes to your rebid. The raise to 2♥ is not a forcing bid. You don't have to bid again when you have a minimum-strength hand. If partner raises your suit to the two level, you pass with minimum values, move toward the game bonus with medium strength, and go right to the game level with maximum values.

Let's see how this works out with each of the following hands. You have opened the bidding 1♥, and your partner has responded 2♥.

♠ 3 2
♥ A Q 8 4 2
♦ Q 7
♣ K J 3 2

You don't want to accept responder's invitation to a game contract, since you hold minimum values. There are 12 high card points and 1 point for the length in the heart suit— a total of 13 points. You have nothing to add to the conversation. You should pass and end the auction. The partnership will play in a partscore contract.

This makes sense because partner's raise to the two level shows a hand of about 6–10 points. The partnership has at most 23 combined points—fewer than the 26 points needed for a game level contract.

♠ 3 2
♥ A Q 8 6 4 2
♦ K Q
♣ K J 3

This hand has 15 high card points plus 2 points for the six-card suit. This gives you 17 points, a medium-strength hand. You'd like to pursue responder's invitation to game by moving toward the game level without actually bidding it. Responder's raise to the two level shows a hand worth about 6–10 points. If responder has only 6–8 points, there won't be enough combined strength for a game level contract. If responder has 9 or 10 points, there should be enough for the game bonus. Move toward the game level by rebidding 3♥, leaving the final decision up to partner. You're sending responder the message that you have some extra values, and if responder also has some extra values, you want to be at the game level.

♠ 3 2
♥ A K Q 6 4 2
♦ K Q
♣ K J 3

Add another 3 points, and you now have 20 points. This is a strong hand, and even if responder has as few as 6 points, there should be enough combined strength for the game. Accept responder's invitation and rebid 4♥.

Responder Makes a Stronger Invitation

"I'd really like to go out to that fish restaurant tonight." Sometimes, your partner makes a strong invitation. Responder make a stronger invitation by jumping a level in support of your opening bid. Suppose you start with 1♥, and responder jumps to 3♥. This response is often used to agree on hearts as a trump suit and to show 11 or 12 points, inviting you to consider the game contract.*

Using your calculator, add the points in your hand to 11 or 12. If you arrive at 26 or more combined points, bid game. If you arrive at fewer than 26 combined points, pass. As an example, suppose partner makes an invitational raise to 3♥ after you open the bidding 1♥ with this hand:

♠ 3 2
♥ A Q 8 4 2
♦ Q 7
♣ K J 3 2

With only 12 high card points and 1 point for the five-card suit, you have the fewest you could hold for an opening bid. Pass, and reject the invitation. Suppose, instead, you hold this hand:

♠ 3 2
♥ A Q 8 4 2
♦ A 7
♣ K J 3 2

*Some partnerships prefer to treat the jump raise of opener's suit as a forcing bid, showing 13 or more points.

Now your hand is worth 15 points. With partner promising at least 11 points, you have enough to accept the invitation and continue on to 4♥.

That's the general idea when partner makes an invitational bid. Add the number of points you hold to those promised by partner's response and decide if there's enough combined strength to accept the invitation.

When partner makes an invitational raise after you've opened a minor suit, and you're planning to accept the invitation, always consider playing the contract in 3NT rather than 5♣ or 5♦. 3NT requires only nine tricks to give you the game bonus. In a minor suit, you have to take eleven tricks before you get the bonus. For example, suppose you open the bidding 1♣ with this hand, and your partner raises to 2♣:

♠ Q 4 2
♥ K Q
♦ K 7
♣ A K J 7 3 2

You have 18 high card points plus 2 points for the six-card suit. 20 points puts this hand in the maximum range, and you should accept partner's invitation. Rather than rebidding 5♣, however, a better choice is 3NT. You should have an easier time taking nine tricks without a trump suit than taking eleven tricks with clubs as the trump suit.

Responder Invites by Bidding Notrump

A response of 1NT shows a hand of about 6–10 points without support for the suit you suggested with your opening bid. Responder doesn't have another suit that can be introduced at the one level. This is an invitational response, and opener doesn't have to bid again if 1NT sounds like the best spot for the partnership.

The principle of the Three Bears is still in place. If you have minimum strength, bid in a minimum fashion; with medium strength, bid "mediumishly"; with a strong hand, bid strongly and get to the game level. As far as the shape of your hand is concerned, you can suggest another trump suit, rebid your own suit, or accept the suggestion to play in notrump.

Let's look at some examples after the bidding has started in this manner:

WEST	NORTH	EAST	SOUTH
	(YOU)		(PARTNER)
	1♥	Pass	1NT
Pass	?		

♠ A 8 7
♥ K J 10 9 3
♦ J 2
♣ K J 6   *minimum*

Partner didn't show support for hearts as the trump suit, and you have a balanced hand and no other suit to suggest as trumps. It sounds as though notrump is the best place to play the contract. You have 13 high card points plus 1 point for the length in the heart suit. That's a minimum-strength hand, so you want to take the minimum action. Since partner's response is not forcing, you can pass and leave the contract in 1NT.

This makes sense because you have 14 points, and partner is showing at most 10 points. There isn't enough combined strength for the partnership to consider a game contract.

♠ 7
♥ K J 10 9 3
♦ J 2
♣ A K J 8 6

Here you have a second suit to suggest. Rebid 2♣, giving partner a choice between clubs and hearts as the trump suit.

♠ A 8 7
♥ K J 10 9 3 2
♦ 2
♣ K J 6

This time you have an unbalanced hand but no second suit to suggest. Rebid 2♥, emphasizing to partner that you think hearts will make a good trump suit even though partner has not shown any support for the suit. With a minimum hand, rebid your suit at the lowest available level.

♠ A 8 7
♥ A K J 10 9 3
♦ 2
♣ K J 6

This is similar to the previous example except that you now have a medium-strength hand of 18 points—16 high card points plus 2 points for the six-card suit. Make a "mediumish" sounding rebid of 3♥, rather than 2♥. This lets partner know that you're interested in reaching the game level if partner has more than 6 or 7 points.

♠ A K 7
♥ K J 10 9 3
♦ A 2
♣ K J 6

20 max?

Here you have a balanced hand worth 20 points—19 high card points plus 1 point for the five-card suit. Since partner hasn't supported your heart suit, and you have no other four-card or longer suit to suggest, playing the contract in notrump sounds like a good idea. With a maximum hand, take the partnership all the way to the game level by rebidding 3NT. Partner will get the message. With a minimum balanced hand, you would pass the 1NT response. With a medium-strength hand, you would raise to 2NT, inviting responder to continue to game with a little extra. With a maximum-strength hand, you go right to the game level.

The more you have, the more you bid.

Some partnerships treat the response of 2NT as an invitational bid showing 11–12 points.* When this is the case, you can follow the same principles. Add your points to those promised by partner. If there's enough combined strength, carry on to the game level. Otherwise, stop in partscore.

Summary

When choosing a rebid, opener classifies the hand as small, medium or large and bids accordingly. A minimum-strength hand is 13–16 points; a medium hand is 17–18 points, and a large hand is 19–21 points. Opener then chooses the rebid that best describes both the strength of the hand and the shape of the hand to partner.

With minimum values, opener rebids as inexpensively as possible; moving cautiously up the bidding levels or passing if responder has made an invitational bid. With medium values, opener can move more vigorously, jumping a level. With maximum values, opener can go all the way to the game level.

Opener must pay attention to the signal that responder is sending. A response in a new suit is a forcing bid, and opener must bid again. If responder raises opener's suit to the two level or bids 1NT, opener doesn't have to bid again because these are invitational bids.

*Some partnerships prefer to use the 2NT response as a forcing bid. You'll need to check with your partner on the preferred style.

new suit bid = forcing
raise bid = invitational

Exercises

1. Categorize the strength of each of the following hands as minimum, medium, or maximum:

a) ♠ K 3
♥ A K 9 7
♦ A K J 3
♣ Q 9 3

b) ♠ 2
♥ A 7 6 3
♦ K 10
♣ A 10 7 6 5 4

c) ♠ A K J 2
♥ A K J 10 8
♦ 9 6
♣ 8 4

2. What would be your choice of rebid with each of the following hands after the auction has started:

WEST	NORTH (YOU)	EAST	SOUTH (PARTNER)
	1♥	Pass	1♠
Pass	?		

a) ♠ 8 4
♥ K Q 10 9 7 3
♦ 10 3
♣ A Q 5

b) ♠ Q 2
♥ A J 8 7 5
♦ A 10 5
♣ Q 9 6

c) ♠ 3
♥ Q J 9 8 4
♦ A K 9 6
♣ K 7 5

d) ♠ K J 7 3
♥ Q 10 8 7 4
♦ A 3
♣ K 10

e) ♠ A J 8 5
♥ A Q 7 6 3
♦ 10
♣ K J 8

f) ♠ 10 9 6 2
♥ A K Q 9 3
♦ —
♣ A K 8 2

g) ♠ 3
♥ A Q 10 9 7 5 2
♦ K Q 6
♣ K 8

h) ♠ 2
♥ A J 9 4 2
♦ A 3
♣ K 10 8 7 4

i) ♠ A 2
♥ A K J 10 9 8 3
♦ K Q 9
♣ 4

3. What would be your choice of rebid with each of the following hands after the auction has started:

WEST	NORTH	EAST	SOUTH
	(YOU)		(PARTNER)
	1♠	Pass	2♠
Pass	?		

a) ♠ A K Q 8 6 2
♥ K 9
♦ A J 8 2
♣ 5

b) ♠ K J 9 8 3
♥ A 10 6 4
♦ 10 5
♣ K J

c) ♠ Q J 9 7 6 4
♥ K 10
♦ A K Q
♣ 8 5

Answers to Exercises

1a) Maximum. This hand contains 20 high card points, putting it in the maximum-strength range of 19–21 points.

1b) Minimum. There are 11 high card points plus 2 points for the six-card suit. That puts this hand into the minimum range, 13–16.

1c) Medium. 16 high card points plus 1 point for the five-card suit puts this hand in the medium-strength category of 17–18 points.

2a) 2♥. This is a minimum, unbalanced hand of 13 points. With no second suit to suggest and without support for partner's suit, rebid your suit at the cheapest possible level.

2b) 1NT. There are 13 high card points plus 1 point for the five-card suit. You can show your minimum-strength, balanced hand by rebidding 1NT.

2c) 2♦. This is a minimum-strength hand. Partner hasn't shown support for your first suit, and you don't like partner's suggested choice of trump suit. Show your other suit to give partner a choice. With a minimum-strength hand, show your suit at the cheapest available level.

2d) 2♠. With four cards in the suit partner has bid, you can agree on spades as the trump suit. The hand is worth 13 high card points and 1 dummy point for each of the doubletons—since you're planning to support partner's suit. With a minimum hand, raise partner to the two level.

2e) 3♠. With support for partner's suit, you can count 3 dummy points for the singleton diamond to go along with your 15 high card points. 18 points puts the hand in the medium-strength category. Show the strength and the support by jumping to the three level when raising partner's suit.

2f) 4♠. Although there are only 16 high card points, you can count 5 dummy points for the void in clubs when planning to raise partner's suit. 21 points puts the hand in the maximum category, and you should raise all the way to the game level.

2g) 3♥. This is a medium-strength hand with 14 high card points plus 3 points for the seven-card suit. With an unbalanced hand, no support for partner's suit, and no second suit to show, rebid your suit with a jump to show the extra strength.

2h) **2♣.** Show your second suit to give partner a choice of trump suits. With a minimum hand of 12 high card points plus 1 point for each of the five-card suits, show your second suit at the cheapest available level.

2i) **4♥.** This is a maximum-strength hand of 20 points—17 high card points plus 3 points for the seven-card suit. That's enough to go right to the game level on your rebid.

3a) **4♠.** There are 17 high card points plus 2 points for the six-card suit, putting this hand in the maximum category. Now that the trump suit has been agreed upon, take the partnership to the game level.

3b) **Pass.** With a minimum-strength hand of 12 high card points plus 1 point for the five-card suit, you don't have to bid any more over partner's invitational response. Partner's raise shows 6–10 points, so the partnership has at most 23 combined points—not enough for game.

3c) **3♠.** There are 15 high card points and 2 points for the six-card suit. This hand falls in the medium-strength category of 17–18 points. Move toward the game level by rebidding 3♠, inviting responder to carry on to game with a little extra.

R&R—Rebids and the Responder

*"O Captain! my Captain! our fearful trip is done,
The ship has weathered every rack, the prize we
sought is won,
The port is near, the bells I hear, the people are
exulting."*

— WALT WHITMAN,
O Captain! My Captain!

When the bidding comes back to responder, it's about time to wind up the conversation and come to a decision about the best contract for the partnership. Opener has made a bid, responder has replied, and opener has made a rebid further describing the hand. Responder usually has enough information to decide on the contract.

If the bidding conversation gets too long, games that you play on your own, like Solitaire, might have a magnetic pull for you. So, let's keep the guidelines as straightforward as possible.

Putting Two and Two Together

Partner has opened the bidding, and you responded. Then opener rebid, and now it's back to you. You have to make your second bid in the auction—*responder's rebid.* You're usually back to being captain. You want to add up the combined strength of the two hands and put that together with the combined distribution to decide on the best contract for the partnership. Let's see how you can figure out both pieces of the puzzle.

The Combined Strength

Listen to the bidding. You can usually tell by listening to the sound of the auction whether opener's hand is small, medium, or large.

OPENER	RESPONDER
1♥	1♠
4♠	?

Wow, that was almost yelling—in the nicest of ways of course. Doesn't it sound as though opener has a maximum-strength hand? The jump all the way to the game bonus level of 4♠ shows the upper range for an opening bid at the one level, about 19–21 points. Here are two other strong-sounding auctions:

OPENER	RESPONDER		OPENER	RESPONDER
1♥	1♠		1♦	1NT
4♥	?		3NT	?

When opener jumps to the game level, you can assume opener has about 20 points. That will help you make a decision.

Now, listen to this auction:

OPENER	RESPONDER
1♥	1♠
2♠	?

Almost a whisper, wasn't it? Opener had to bid again because a new suit by responder is forcing. Opener raised your suit as cheaply as possible. Opener is showing a minimum-strength hand of about 13–16 points. Here are two more whispers:

min.
14-15
2 level
①

OPENER	RESPONDER		OPENER	RESPONDER
1♥	1♠	*14-15*	1♥	1♠
2♥	?		1NT	?

When opener makes a rebid that sounds like a whisper, you can assume that opener has about 14 or 15 points.

Finally, listen to this auction:

med.
17-18

OPENER	RESPONDER
1♥	1♠
3♠	?

Not too soft, and not too loud. Sounds like a medium-strength hand of about 17 or 18 points—too much to make a quiet raise to 2♠; not quite enough to jump all the way to the game level. Here are two more medium-sounding bids:

min
Pass or
game
may

OPENER	RESPONDER *6-10*		OPENER	RESPONDER
1♥	1♠		1♥	2♥
3♥	?		3♥	?

In the last auction, opener could have passed your invitational raise with a minimum hand or gone right to the game level with a maximum hand. Sounds medium to me.

The Combined Fit

Figuring out if there's a suitable eight-card or longer trump suit also comes from listening to opener's description of the hand. Listen to this:

13-21 ?
min.

OPENER	RESPONDER *6-10 ?*
1♥	1♠
2♠	?

No trouble here. The partnership has found a spade fit. The only decision left for responder is whether or not there's enough combined strength to go for the game bonus. Now listen to this auction:

OPENER	RESPONDER
1♣	1♦
1NT	?

Opener is showing a balanced hand. It's unlikely that the partnership has a major suit fit because opener didn't rebid 1♥ or 1♠ to show a four-card suit. Try this auction:

OPENER	RESPONDER
1♥	1♠
2♥	?

*no S support
6+ H*

Opener is describing a hand with a long heart suit, probably six or more cards. Opener doesn't have support for your spade suit, doesn't have a balanced hand, and doesn't have another suit to suggest.

Making a Decision

Responder wants to get the partnership to the best partscore or to a bonus level whenever possible. If there are fewer than 26 combined points, your target is to play at the partscore level in a suitable trump fit or in notrump. With 26 or more combined points, you want to make sure the partnership ends up in one of the game level contracts. If you're lucky enough to have 33 or more combined points, you have the opportunity to go for a slam bonus.

Settling for Partscore

Sometimes both opener and responder have minimum values. It's time to stop in partscore. When opener shows a minimum hand and responder has about 6–10 points, responder must be cautious. It's no time to be introducing another new suit. Instead, responder

should choose one of the suits that have already been mentioned or
settle for a 1NT partscore. Let's look at some examples.

OPENER	RESPONDER
♠ K 8 6	♠ J 10 4
♥ 9 4	♥ Q J 8 6
♦ A Q J 6 5	♦ K 3
♣ A 6 3	♣ 10 9 5 2

1♦	*I like diamonds and have 13–21 points.*	1♥	*I have at least four hearts and at least 6 points. I expect you to bid again.*
13-15 1NT	*I have a balanced hand with 13–15 points and I don't have support for your hearts.*	Pass	*This is no time to go higher or look for some other trump fit. Let's settle for partscore in notrump.*

OPENER	RESPONDER
♠ A 7 3	♠ J 10 4
13 ♥ 10 5	♥ Q J 8 6 5 2 *9*
♦ A J 6 5	♦ K 3
♣ A 6 4 3	♣ 10 9

1♦	*I like diamonds and have 13–21 points.*	1♥	*I have at least four hearts and at least 6 points. I expect you to bid again.*
1NT	*I have a balanced hand with 13–15 points, and I don't have support for your hearts.*	2♥	*If you've got a balanced hand, you must have at least two cards in the heart suit. We don't have enough combined strength for a game contract, so let's settle for partscore with hearts as trump. I expect you to pass.*

13

OPENER	RESPONDER
♠ K Q J	♠ 10 4
♥ 8 2	♥ Q J 8 6 5
♦ Q J 6 2	♦ K 10 9 5 3
♣ A 10 7 3	♣ 2

	OPENER		RESPONDER
1♦	*I like diamonds and have 13–21 points.*	1♥	*How do you feel about hearts as a trump suit?*
1NT	*I have a balanced hand with 13–15 points, and I don't have support for your hearts.*	2♦	*I like your diamonds. I didn't tell you right away because I was hoping we had a major suit fit. Let's play partscore with diamonds as trump. I expect you to pass.*

This last hand illustrates why responder can afford to look for a major suit fit even when there's a known minor suit fit. Rather than showing the diamond support right away, responder looks for a heart fit and then goes back to the diamond suit when no major suit fit is found.

OPENER	RESPONDER
♠ A 8 6	♠ 10 8
♥ 9 4	♥ Q J 8 6 5
♦ A K J 10 6 5	♦ 5 3
♣ K 6	♣ Q 8 7 2

	OPENER		RESPONDER
1♦	*I like diamonds and have 13–21 points.*	1♥	*Tell me more.*
3♦	*I have an unbalanced hand with 17–18 points. I don't have support for your hearts, but I do have a lot of diamonds.*	Pass	*Nice to hear you have a medium-strength hand, but I think we should settle for partscore.*

Considering the Game Level

Suppose opener shows a hand in the minimum range of 13–16 points, and responder has about 11 or 12 points. There might not be enough combined strength for the game level if opener is at the very bottom of the range. On the other hand, if opener has a little extra, perhaps 15 or 16 points, the partnership will have the 26 points needed to go for the game bonus.

With 11 or 12 points, responder doesn't want to settle for partscore but can't afford to take the partnership all the way to the game level. Instead, responder moves toward the game level without quite getting there. This sends opener an invitation: carry on to game with a little extra; otherwise, pass.

Let's see how this works.

OPENER	RESPONDER
♠ Q 6	♠ K J 9 4
♥ J 9 4 3	♥ Q 10 5
♦ A J 9 2	♦ 6 4 3
♣ K Q 3	♣ A J 8

1♦   *I have a diamond suit and enough strength to open the bidding.*

                                     1♠   *I have at least four spades and at least 6 points. I expect you to bid again.*

1NT   *I have a balanced hand with 13–15 points, but I can't support for your spade suit.*

                                       2NT   *Since you don't like my spades, it sounds as though notrump is the best denomination. I've got too much to give up on the game bonus but not quite enough to bid 3NT myself. Do you have anything extra?*

Pass   *Sorry. I'd like to accept the invitation, but I've got only the 13 points I started with. Hope we aren't too high.*

OPENER
- ♠ J 7
- ♥ A 9 6
- ♦ A K 10 6 5
- ♣ Q 10 5

RESPONDER
- ♠ K Q 10 9 5 4
- ♥ 10 3
- ♦ 6 4
- ♣ A J 8

1♦ *I've got at least 13 points, enough to start the bidding.*

1♠ *I've got four or more spades and 6 or more points. I expect to hear more about your hand.*

1NT *My hand is balanced, with 13–15 points. Not enough to open 1NT originally. I don't have enough spades to raise your suit.*

3♠ *With 12 points, I'm too strong to sign off in partscore but not strong enough to go to game by myself. Since you must have at least two spades, we've got an eight-card fit. What do you think?*

4♠ *My spade support isn't that great, but I do have the top of the range for my 1NT rebid. I'm going to accept your invitation. Good luck!*

OPENER
- ♠ A 5
- ♥ A 7 4
- ♦ K Q 7 5
- ♣ 10 8 6 3

RESPONDER
- ♠ K J 9 4
- ♥ 10 5
- ♦ A J 6 4 2
- ♣ J 8

1♦ *Another opening bid. This is getting to be a habit.*

1♠ *Let's see if we've got a spade fit. I can always support diamonds later.*

1NT *Sorry, I can't support your spades. I've got a balanced hand in the 13–15 point range.*

3♦ *Better let you know about my diamond support. At the same time, I want to invite you to continue to*

*game, since I've got a
hand in the 11–12 point
range.*

Pass   *Thanks for the invitation,
but with only 13 points, I
think I'll decline and
settle for partscore in our
diamond fit.*

That's the general idea for responder with 11–12 points after opener shows a minimum-strength hand. Bid 2NT, or rebid one of the partnership suits at the three level, inviting opener to carry on.

If opener shows a medium or maximum hand when responder has 11–12 points, the partnership should always get to at least the game bonus level. The partnership has more than the 26 combined points needed for the game level, and responder may even consider going for the slam bonus. More on that later.

Going for the Game Bonus

Once responder has 13 or more points, there's no stopping in partscore. The combined partnership strength is at least 26 points, and responder should be targeting the best game level contract. Listen to these auctions.

OPENER
♠ Q 10 6
♥ A 4
♦ K Q 10 7 3
♣ J 10 3

RESPONDER *13*
♠ J 9 3
♥ K Q 8 3
♦ A J 9
♣ Q 7 5

1♦   *I've got enough to open
the bidding, but I don't
have the right hand to
start with 1NT.*

1♥   *What do you think about
hearts as a trump suit?*

1NT   *I can't support your
hearts, but I can tell you
I've got a balanced hand
with 13–15 points.*

3NT   *I've got 13 points, so we
must have enough com-
bined strength for the game
level. We haven't uncov-*

ered an eight-card major
suit fit, so notrump looks
like the spot. I'm putting
the partnership in the best
game contract.

Pass   *You're the captain.*

OPENER
♠ K 10 2
♥ 10 4
♦ K Q 6 5
♣ A J 10 3

RESPONDER
♠ 3
♥ K Q J 9 8 3
♦ A J 9
♣ Q 7 5

1♦   *It must be nice to have a partner that keeps opening the bidding!*

1♥   *I better let partner know about my heart suit. I'll wait to hear partner's rebid before deciding on a contract.*

1NT   *Another minimum balanced hand. I never seem to have support for your suit.*

4♥   *I don't need to hear anymore. I've got a hand worth 15 points, so we must belong at the game level. Partner must have at least two hearts, so we've got a suitable eight-card major suit fit. I can't rebid 2♥; that would ask partner to pass. I can't rebid 3♥; that's an invitation, and partner might not accept. I'll have to take command and put the partnership in a game contract.*

Pass   *Good luck. Hope I've got what you expect.*

Step by Step

There's more than one way to get to the game level. One of my students asked me if the following auction made any sense:

OPENER	RESPONDER
1♥	2♥
3♥	4♥

I replied that I thought the partnership had a lot of heart. In fact, the auction makes very good sense. The partnership hands might be something like this:

OPENER
- ♠ A Q 6
- ♥ A Q 9 7 5 3
- ♦ Q 5
- ♣ Q 3

RESPONDER
- ♠ K 8 2
- ♥ 10 6 4 2
- ♦ K 3
- ♣ K 9 6 2

1♥ *I have a hand with hearts, somewhere in the range of 13–21 points.*

3♥ *I've got a medium-strength hand of 17–18 points—too much to pass and leave the partnership in partscore, too little to go all the way to the game level.*

Pass *Now that we've bid to the game level, I hope I can make the contract!*

2♥ *I have 6–10 points and support for your heart suit.*

4♥ *I've got 9 HCPs plus 1 dummy point for the doubleton diamond. That puts me at the top of my 6–10 range. I'm going to go for the bonus.*

Going for Bigger Things

Sometimes, responder will add up the combined points and reach a total of 33 points or more. Now it's time to consider venturing beyond the game level and into the slam zone. For example, look at these auctions.

15

OPENER	RESPONDER
♠ K 8 6	♠ A Q 3
♥ Q 8	♥ A K J 10 9
♦ A 10 8 7 2	♦ 6 4
♣ K Q 4	♣ A J 5

1♦   *I've got at least 13 points, enough to open the bidding.*

1♥   *Do you like hearts as a trump suit? I certainly hope you remember that my response is forcing.*

1NT   *I'd better finish describing my hand. It's balanced, and I'm at the lower end of the 13–12 point range.*

6NT   *I've got 20 points—19 high card points plus 1 for the five-card suit—and partner has at least 13. That gives us at least 33 combined points. Partner hasn't show any interest in playing with hearts as the trump suit, so I'm going to take the partnership to the slam zone. Here goes.*

Pass   *Whoa! That was little unexpected. If I can make this contract, we'll have a good story after the game.*

13

OPENER	RESPONDER
♠ K 7 4	♠ —
♥ 9 4	♥ A K J 10 9
♦ K Q 7 3	♦ A J 8 6 2
♣ A J 6 2	♣ K 10 8

1♦   *Another quiet opening bid at the one level.*

1♥   *I like diamonds, but I'm going to check for a major suit fit first.*

1NT   *I don't have anything extra partner, just that*

6♦   *This should be fun. I've got 16 high card points*

same old minimum
balanced hand.

and good support for
partner's diamonds. I can
count 5 dummy points for
the spade void. Even if
partner has a minimum
for the opening bid, we
should have a good shot at
taking twelve tricks.

Pass   *I hope I'm not supposed to
bid any more with this
hand. Partner certainly
has a lot of faith in the
way I play the hands.*

There are fancier ways to reach the slam level, but simply adding up the combined points and blasting into a contract at the six level is lots of fun and will usually put the partnership in the best spot.

Summary

When it's time for responder to make a rebid, enough information has usually been passed back and forth for responder to make a decision about the contract. Responder plays the role of captain, directing the partnership to the best contract.

The points shown by opener are added to those in responder's hand. If the total is fewer than 26, responder puts the partnership in a partscore contract. When there are 26 or more, responder puts the partnership in a game level contract. Occasionally, the total will be 33 or more, and the partnership can go for a big bonus by bidding to the slam level.

In deciding on the best contract, responder listens to opener's description of the hand. If the partnership has uncovered a suitable trump fit, responder uses that information when choosing the contract. If no suitable trump suit has been found, responder guides the partnership into a notrump contract.

Exercises

1. What would you rebid with each of the following hands after the auction starts off: *captain*

OPENER	RESPONDER
1♣	1♠
2♣	?

min strength level

a) ♠ K J 8 4 3
  ♥ Q 9 5
  ♦ 6 4
  ♣ J 10 4

8   *pass*

b) ♠ K J 8 4 3
  ♥ Q 9 5
  ♦ 6 4
  ♣ K J 10

11   *3♠*

c) ♠ K J 8 4 3
  ♥ A 9 5
  ♦ 6 4
  ♣ K J 10

13   *4♠*

2. What would you rebid with each of the following hands in this auction:

OPENER	RESPONDER
1♥	1♠
2♥	?

Responder   *13*   *at least 6 H*

a) ♠ A J 7 5
  ♥ A 6
  ♦ 7 5 2
  ♣ A 10 4 3

b) ♠ K Q 10 5
  ♥ 5
  ♦ A Q 6 2
  ♣ K J 8 4

3 NT

c) ♠ Q J 9 5
  ♥ 6 2
  ♦ Q 10 7 4
  ♣ J 9 6

6   *Pass*

3. What would you do with each of the following hands after the auction begins:

OPENER	RESPONDER
1♦	1♠
3♣	?

17-18

a) ♠ Q 9 6 3
  ♥ 9 5 4
  ♦ J 6
  ♣ K 8 6 4

6   *Pass*

b) ♠ A 10 9 6
  ♥ 9 5 4
  ♦ J 6
  ♣ K 8 6 4

8   *4♠*

c) ♠ A Q 10 8 4 3
  ♥ A 9 3
  ♦ 4
  ♣ A J 9

17   *6♠*

Answers to Exercises

1a) **Pass**. Partner's raise to 2♠ shows a minimum-strength hand of 13–16 points. You have 7 high card points plus 1 point for the fifth spade. That's not enough combined strength to go for the game bonus. Pass, and play in a partscore contract.

1b) **3♠**. Your hand falls into the 11–12 point range—10 high card points plus 1 for the five-card suit. Even though opener has shown a minimum hand, there may still be enough for the game bonus. Move toward the game level, inviting opener to carry on with a little extra.

1c) **4♠**. You have 13 points—12 high card points plus 1 for the five-card suit. Go for the game bonus in the agreed trump suit.

2a) **4♥**. With 13 points, you know the partnership should reach the game level. Partner has bid hearts twice, rather than supporting your suit or showing another suit. It sounds as though partner has at least six of them. Bid game in the eight-card major suit fit.

2b) **3NT**. You again have enough to put the partnership in a game level contract. With no liking for partner's suggested trump suit, try for the nine-trick bonus contract of 3NT.

2c) **Pass**. You have only 6 points, and partner is showing a minimum hand. Time to stop bidding.

3a) **Pass**. Partner's jump raise is invitational, showing about 17–18 points and support for your suit. With only 6 points, reject partner's invitation, and settle for partscore.

3b) **4♠**. With 9 points, you have enough to accept the invitation. Even if partner has only 17, there will be 26 combined points.

3c) **6♠**. Partner is showing 17 or 18 points and you have 17–15 high card points plus 2 for the six-card suit. That's a minimum of 34 combined points. Go for the big bonus.

♣ ♦ ♥ ♠ ♣ ♦ ♥ ♠ ♣ ♦ ♥ ♠ **10** ♣ ♦ ♥ ♠ ♣ ♦ ♥ ♠ ♣ ♦ ♥ ♠ ♣

Hints for the Declarer

> *"It looked insanely complicated, and this was one*
> *of the reasons why the snug plastic cover it fitted*
> *into had the words DON'T PANIC printed on*
> *it in large friendly letters."*
>
> —DOUGLAS ADAMS,
> *The Hitchhiker's Guide to the Galaxy*

The auction is over; the opening lead is made. Partner puts down the dummy face up on the table. All of a sudden, you find yourself as declarer, and it's up to you to make the contract for your side. Don't panic.

Planning the Play

The first thing you should do, before choosing a card to play from the dummy, is to take a moment to think about how many tricks you need to make the contract. Add six to the level of your contract. If you're in a contract of 2♥, you have to take 6 + 2 = 8 tricks. In a contract of 3NT, you have to take 6 + 3 = 9 tricks; in a contract of 7♦, you have to take all thirteen of the tricks.

The next step is to see how close you are to being successful in your contract. You do this by counting your *sure tricks*, or *winners*— the tricks you can take without giving the lead to the opponents. Australian writer Paul Marston refers to these as *certain tricks*. That has a nice ring to it. Look at each suit in turn. For example, suppose these are the spades you can see in both hands:

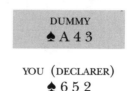

DUMMY
♠ A 4 3

YOU (DECLARER)
♠ 6 5 2

The cards in the dummy have been shaded to remind you that they're the ones face up on the table. When you first look at this suit, you see no sure tricks in your hand. Look across at the dummy, and there's one sure trick, the ace. Now take a look at another suit:

DUMMY
♥ Q 6 4

YOU
♥ A K 2

You have the two highest cards in the suit, and when you look across at the dummy, your side has the third highest card in the suit. You have three winners in this suit. Be careful when counting your sure tricks. Suppose this is the diamond suit:

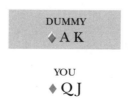

DUMMY
♦ A K

YOU
♦ Q J

You have all four of the high cards in the suit, but this translates into only two sure tricks. Since you have only two cards on each side of the table, you can play the suit only twice—you can't take more tricks than that.

It's interesting that a card as low as a two could give you an extra trick. Consider this suit:

DUMMY

♦ A K 2

YOU

♦ Q 3

In this example, you can take three tricks, with one less high card. You can win the first trick with the ♦Q, playing the ♦2 from the dummy. Then, you can play the ♦3 over to dummy's ♦A and ♦K.

Your sure tricks don't come only from the high cards. Consider this suit:

DUMMY

♣ 6 5 4 3 2

YOU

♣ A K Q 8 7

You have the three top cards in the suit, and you also have ten clubs in the combined hands. There are only thirteen cards in each suit, so the defenders have a total of three clubs. By the time you have played the first three tricks in the suit, the opponents won't have any clubs left. You can keep on taking tricks and will end up with five sure tricks.

The exercise of counting your sure tricks will provide you with some useful information. Either you'll have enough tricks to make your contract—and all you have to do is take them—or you'll fall short and need to look for ways of getting the extra tricks you need. We'll take a look at both situations.

How to Take Your Sure Tricks

This sounds like a contradiction of terms. A sure thing is a sure thing. But remember the story of the dog who was walking across the bridge with a bone in its mouth—a sure thing. The dog caught its reflection in the clear water and went for the additional bone, dropping his sure thing. What a shame.

Here are a few tips to help declarer take those sure tricks.

Take Your Tricks and Run

Suppose you reach a contract of 3NT, and the opening lead is the ♥K. This is what you see when the dummy comes down:

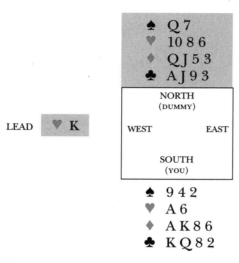

You need nine tricks to make your contract of 3NT. You don't have any sure tricks in spades, but you do have one sure trick in the heart suit. You can also take four tricks from the diamond suit and four tricks from the club suit, since you have the top four cards in each suit. That's a total of nine. Time to take your tricks and run. Win the first trick with the ♥A, take your four diamond tricks and four club tricks, and let the defenders take the rest.

What could go wrong? Nothing, provided you win the first trick and take your tricks right away. If you didn't win the first trick, however, or you led some suit other than clubs or diamonds before taking your nine tricks, the defenders could defeat your contract. They might take five or more tricks from the heart suit and the spade suit. Remember, they're not on your side. They're trying to take enough tricks to defeat the contract.

Entries

Take a look at this suit:

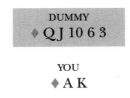

DUMMY
♦ Q J 10 6 3

YOU
♦ A K

You have all the top cards in the suit, and it might seem as though there are five sure tricks. You can take tricks with the ♦A and ♦K, playing the two low diamonds from dummy's hand. You have the ♦Q, ♦J, and ♦10 left in the dummy for three more tricks. The problem with all this is that you have to lead from the hand that won the last trick. After taking the first two tricks, you're still in your hand and can't lead dummy's good diamonds.

You can't call a taxi to get from one side of the table to another. You need an *entry*. Suppose we change the layout of the diamond suit to look like this:

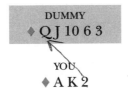

DUMMY
♦ Q J 10 6 3

YOU
♦ A K 2

That little ♦2 becomes a big star. After winning the first two tricks with the ace and king, you can use the ♦2 as an entry to travel across to the dummy and take three more tricks. If you didn't have the ♦2, you would have to find an entry to the dummy in some other suit. That will often be possible, but the order in which you take your sure tricks is important.

Try laying out the following complete deal on the table. You're South and are the declarer in a 1NT contract. West leads the ♠Q. See if you can make your contract.

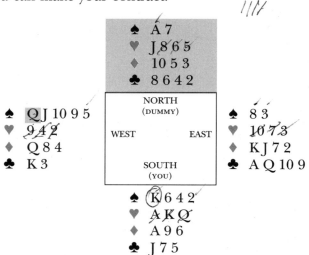

You need to win seven tricks to make the contract. Count your sure tricks. There are two spade tricks, the ♠A and ♠K. There are four heart tricks because your side has the four top cards in the suit. There's one diamond trick, the ace. That's a total of seven tricks. All you have to do is be careful with the order in which you take them. You have an important decision to make on the very first trick.

You could win the first trick with either the ♠A in the dummy or the ♠K in your hand. This is a critical choice. Suppose you win the first trick with dummy's ♠A. Next you lead a low heart and win the trick with the ♥A. You can then take the ♥K, ♥Q, ♠K, and ♦A, but there's no way to reach dummy's hand to lead the ♥J—no taxi!

Instead, win the first trick with the ♠K in your hand, and leave the ♠A in the dummy until later. You then take the three top hearts and the ♦A. Finally, you play a low spade and win the trick with dummy's carefully preserved ♠A. You're in the right hand to lead the ♥J, your seventh trick. The ♠A was the entry you needed to get from your hand over to the dummy.

Try this hand. This time, you're in a contract of 3NT, and you need to take nine tricks to be successful. The opening lead from West is the ♦K.

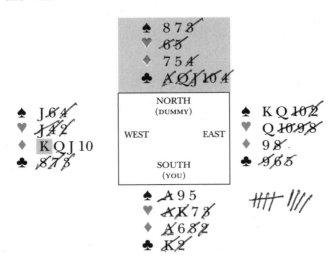

You appear to have the nine sure tricks you need: there's one spade trick, the ace; there are two heart tricks, the ace and king; there's the ♦A; and you have the five top cards in the club suit. Be careful. The order in which you take your tricks is still important.

After winning a trick with the ♦A, suppose you start taking your club tricks from the top down—winning the first trick with dummy's ♣A and the next with your ♣K. Taxi time again. You're in your hand, and there's no way to get over to the dummy to play your three remaining club winners.

There's a useful guideline when taking tricks in a suit that doesn't have the same number of cards on both sides of the table:

• Play the high card(s) from the short side first.

You have the shortness in the club suit. Play your ♣K first and then the ♣2 over to dummy's ace. Now you're in the right place at the right time. You can take three more club tricks and play your other aces and kings to make the contract.

Drawing Trump

Trump cards are valuable, since a low trump can overpower the ace in another suit. But it's a double-edged sword. The defenders can also make use of the trump suit if you aren't careful. Here's an example. The contract is 4♠, and you're the declarer sitting South. The opening lead is the ♥A.

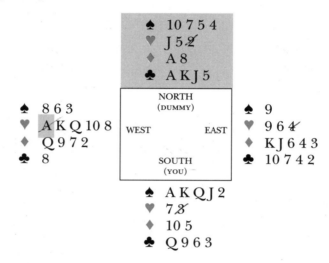

West wins the first trick with the ♥A, the second trick with the ♥K, and then tries to win a third trick with the ♥Q. You can see the importance of playing with a trump suit because you're able to win this trick by playing the ♠2 from your hand. It looks as if you have the ten tricks you need to make the 4♠ contract: five spade tricks, the ♦A, and four club tricks. Can anything go wrong?

Suppose you start by taking your club tricks. On the second round of the suit, West has no clubs left and can play the ♠3, winning the trick for the defense. One of your sure tricks has suddenly disappeared. You'll end up one trick short of making your contract.

There's a way to prevent this and, as usual, it has to do with the order in which you take your tricks. Instead of trying to take your club tricks right away, start by taking tricks in the trump suit. You play your ♠A, ♠K, and ♠Q. Now, West has no spades left and can't prevent you from taking all your club tricks and making the contract.

You don't have to take all your spade tricks, only enough to make sure the defenders have none left. This is called *drawing trumps*. You'll have to count how many trumps are left in the defenders' hands. Remember that there are only thirteen cards in each suit. Count the number of trumps your side started with. That tells you how many remain in the defenders' hands. Each time you play the trump suit, watch to see if both defenders follow suit with a trump or whether only one defender plays a trump. You'll soon get used to counting up to thirteen—that's a big part of the game.

You don't always draw the defenders' trumps right away. There are sometimes more important things to do first. However, if you have the number of tricks you need to make the contract, start by drawing trump.

Developing Extra Tricks

The previous hands were all very pleasant to play. You had the tricks you needed. You had only to be careful to take them in the right order. Of course, that won't always be the case. You'll frequently discover that you don't have enough sure tricks to make the contract. There are a number of ways of getting the extra tricks you need. We've already touched on some of them in the chapter *Taking Tricks*. Let's take a closer look. You'll probably find it easier to follow each example if you deal out the cards on the table.

Promotion—Putting Big Cards to Work

Suppose this is the layout of the diamond suit between your hand and the dummy:

DUMMY

◆ 6 5 3 2

YOU

◆ K Q J 10

There are no sure tricks in this suit, but there's lots of potential. By leading this suit, you make the defenders play the ◆A, if they want to win the trick. Your remaining cards have now been *promoted* into sure tricks, and you end up with three diamond tricks.

To promote tricks in a suit, you have to give up the lead to the defenders. This is a common tactic during the play. As long as the defenders can't take enough tricks to defeat the contract when they get the opportunity to lead, you'll end up developing the extra tricks necessary to make the contract. Don't be afraid to give up the lead to the defenders. You don't have to take all your tricks right away. The important thing is to have won enough tricks by the time the hand is over.

Sometimes you have to be patient to promote a trick:

There are no sure tricks. You have to lose two club tricks, to the defenders' ace and king, before you end up promoting a trick in the suit. This may not seem like much of a trade—you have to give up two tricks to get only one—but it may be the extra trick you need to make the contract.

The high cards don't need to be on the same side of the table, and the suit doesn't have to be evenly divided between the two hands:

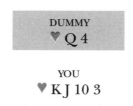

You can promote three tricks in this suit by driving out the defenders' ace. When the suit is unevenly divided between the two hands, use the same guideline as when taking sure tricks: play the high card from the short side first. Start by playing the ♥Q, high card from the short side—either by leading it from the dummy's hand or by leading your ♥3 over to dummy's queen if you're starting from your side.

The reason for this may not be clear at first. Before we discuss this in a little more detail, I should tell you about my yoga class—where I ask too many questions. My instructor says, "Just do it, and the reasons will reveal themselves." Now, I'm not generally a subscriber to such a philosophy, but what harm can there be in trying to breathe a certain way? Before I run out of breath, let's continue our bridge discussion. You're the declarer in a contract of 3NT and have to take nine tricks. The opening lead is the ♠6.

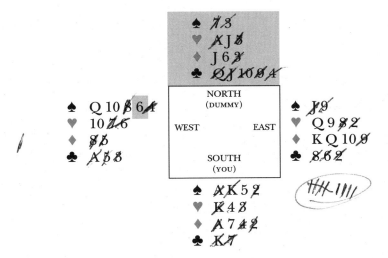

There are a total of five sure tricks: two spades, two hearts, and one diamond trick. You need to find four extra tricks to make your 3NT contract. The club suit provides the potential for the extra tricks through promotion.

Win the first trick with the ♠K or ♠A. Play the ♣K, high card from the short side. If West wins this trick with the ♣A, the rest is easy. Whatever West does next, you can win and play the ♣7 over to dummy and take four club tricks. After taking the rest of your aces and kings, you'll end up with nine tricks. Even if West doesn't win the ♣A right away—West doesn't have to play the ace the first time the suit is led—you can lead another club and continue leading the suit until the ace is gone.

It's important to go after the tricks you have to develop before taking the winners in your other suits. If you start by taking your five sure tricks, and then lead the ♣K, it's too late. The defenders will be able to take enough tricks in the other suits to defeat the contract.

Lead the ♣K right away, while you still have lots of high cards left in the other suit. That way, nothing the defenders do can stop you from making the contract.

Having done your breathing exercise, you may still wonder why you had to start the club suit by playing the king. Lay out the cards again. After winning the first trick, try leading your ♣7 over to dummy's ♣Q and then dummy's ♣4 back to your king. See what happens if West refuses to win either of these tricks with the ♣A. You'll find that you have difficulty ending up with more than two club tricks. You're going to need too many taxis to get over to the dummy.

Length—Putting Little Cards to Work

Take the heart suit from your deck, and lay out the cards like this:

You have two sure tricks in this suit with the ♥A and ♥K. There are no big cards to promote, so you're going to have to work with the little cards if you want an extra trick in this situation. Between your hand and the dummy there are eight cards in the heart suit, leaving the defenders with only five. If the defenders' hearts are divided reasonably between the two hands, one defender will have three hearts, and the other will have two—as in the diagram.

Look what happens if you take the first two tricks in the suit with your ace and king and then lead the suit a third time. The defenders have to follow suit to the first two tricks, but West will be able to win the third trick. Now, however, you have the only remaining hearts. You'll have developed an extra trick in the heart suit. When you regain the lead, play a heart, and both defenders will have to discard—assuming there's no trump suit, or the defenders have no trump left. This technique is referred to as developing extra tricks through the *length* of the suit.

To develop tricks through length, the cards held by the defenders don't necessarily need to be evenly divided, and you might not need to have any high cards in the suit. Suppose the hearts are divided in this fashion:

DUMMY
♥ 9 6 3 2

WEST   EAST
♥ A K J   ♥ Q

YOU
♥ 10 8 7 5 4

You have no sure tricks in this suit, and it may look so weak that you want to turn your eyes elsewhere. Remember, any card that can be turned into a winner ends up with the power of an ace, whether it takes the first trick or the last. If you were to lead this suit three times—every time you have an opportunity—the defenders would take three tricks, but you would end up with the last two tricks in the suit because the defenders would have no hearts left.

Here's a hand to illustrate the point. Once again you're in a contract of 3NT, and this time the opening lead is the ♥J.

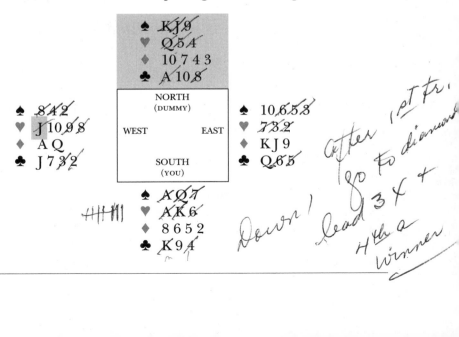

You need to take nine tricks and have three spade tricks, three heart tricks, and two club tricks—a total of eight tricks. You need only one more trick. Look in the most unlikely place. That's right, the diamonds. Win the first trick, and lead diamonds—right away. You'll lose the trick, but the defenders have to give you the next trick because you have lots of strength in the other suits. Now lead another diamond. The defenders take the trick again. Whichever suit they lead, win the trick, and lead diamonds for the third time.

Although the defenders win the third diamond trick, they now have no diamonds left, and your remaining diamonds represent a winning trick. As soon as you regain the lead, lead diamonds for the fourth time. That's your ninth trick—like a rabbit pulled out of the hat.

As a guideline, when you aren't sure where your extra tricks are going to come from, lead the longest suit in the combined hands. You'll often be pleasantly surprised at the results.

The Finesse—Putting Medium-Sized Cards to Work

Be sure to take out your cards for this exercise. Suppose you need to take two tricks from the heart suit in this layout:

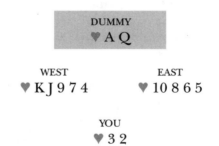

```
                    DUMMY
                   ♥ A Q

      WEST                    EAST
   ♥ K J 9 7 4            ♥ 10 8 6 5

                    YOU
                   ♥ 3 2
```

You have one sure trick with the ♥A. Where's the second trick to come from? You want to make use of the ♥Q. It won't do much good to play the ♥A and then the ♥Q because West will win the second trick with the ♥K. The guideline here is to lead toward the card you hope will take a trick. Start by leading a low heart from your hand toward the dummy, making West play before you have to choose the card to play from the dummy. Suppose, West plays a low heart. You play dummy's ♥Q, and it wins the trick. You still have the ♥A left for a second trick in the suit.

Playing the suit in this fashion is called taking a *finesse*. You're hoping the defenders' cards are favorably located and that your finesse will be successful. That won't always be the case. If the ♥K is moved to East's hand, this will be the layout:

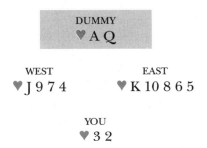

When you lead a low heart toward dummy and play the ♥Q, East will win the trick with the ♥K, and your finesse will lose. Too bad, but there was nothing you could do. Sometimes your finesses work, sometimes they don't.

The finesse comes in many guises and is sometimes a challenge to spot during the play of a hand. Nonetheless, the principle of leading toward a card which you hope will win a trick usually guides you in the right direction. Try your luck with this hand. You have stopped in a partscore of 1NT and need seven tricks to make the contract. The opening lead is the ♦5.

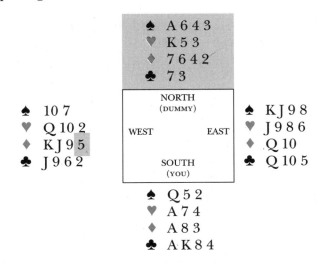

You can count one sure trick in spades, two in hearts, one in diamonds, and two in clubs. You're one trick short if you take all your aces and kings. Where's the seventh trick to come from? The spade suit offers a possibility because you have the queen—a card with which you'd like to win a trick even though the defenders have the king. Let's try it.

After winning a trick with the ♦A, you want to lead toward the ♠Q. You can do this by traveling over to the dummy using the ♣A or ♥K. Then lead a low spade from dummy toward your hand. East has to play next. If East plays the ♠K, winning the trick, you'll save your ♠Q for later. If East doesn't play the ♠K, you play the ♠Q, and your finesse is a success right away. West doesn't have a higher spade to play. Sooner or later, the ♠Q becomes your seventh trick, and you make the contract.

Try playing the spade suit in some other fashion—leading the queen, for example. You'll find that you end up with only one trick from the suit. First you have to spot the opportunity for a finesse, and then you have to be careful which side of the table you lead from. There's lots of excitement waiting to see if it's going to succeed.

Ruffing—Putting the Trump to Work

The trump suit is your friend. Not only can it stop the defenders from winning tricks with their high cards, you can use it to get the extra tricks you need. Consider this hand. You've reached a contract of 4♥, and the opening lead is the ♣K.

4 H

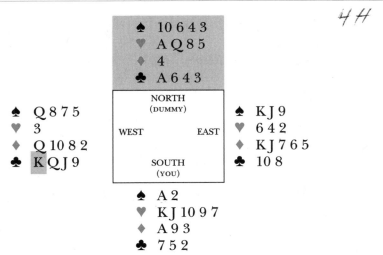

```
                    ♠ 10 6 4 3
                    ♥ A Q 8 5
                    ♦ 4
                    ♣ A 6 4 3
                 ┌─────────────────┐
   ♠ Q 8 7 5     │     NORTH        │   ♠ K J 9
   ♥ 3           │    (DUMMY)       │   ♥ 6 4 2
   ♦ Q 10 8 2    │ WEST      EAST   │   ♦ K J 7 6 5
   ♣ K Q J 9     │                  │   ♣ 10 8
                 │     SOUTH        │
                 │     (YOU)        │
                 └─────────────────┘
                    ♠ A 2
                    ♥ K J 10 9 7
                    ♦ A 9 3
                    ♣ 7 5 2
```

You need to take ten tricks to be successful, and you have a sure spade trick, five heart tricks, one diamond trick, and one club trick. That's only eight tricks. There's nothing much to promote or finesse, and your long suits aren't going to provide you with two extra tricks.

The key here is the singleton diamond in the dummy. It allows you to make use of the trump suit to provide the two extra tricks you need. After winning the ♣A, play the ♦4 and win the trick with your ♦A. Dummy has no diamonds left after this trick, so you can lead another diamond and play one of dummy's trumps to win the trick. That's the first extra trick. Now play a low spade from dummy and win the trick with the ♠A in your hand. Lead your last diamond, and again win the trick by using one of dummy's trumps. That's the second extra trick.

Notice that you still have five heart tricks left to take. In effect, you're going to take seven tricks from the trump suit, rather than five. That's where your extra tricks come from.

Earlier, we discussed drawing trump right away when you have all the tricks you need. That's not the case when you're looking for extra tricks. Sometimes you have to delay playing the trump suit. On this hand, if you were to play the trump suit first, it would take three rounds before East had no hearts left. That would leave you with only one trump in the dummy. You could get one extra trick by trumping—or ruffing—one of your low diamonds in the dummy, but you couldn't get the second extra trick.

There's lots to think about during the play, especially when you have a trump suit. But don't let things get too bogged down. Try something, and see how it works out.

Summary

When you're the declarer, take a moment to remind yourself of the number of tricks you're trying to take to make the contract. Count the sure tricks that you have, and see how close you are to your goal.

If you have the tricks you need, take them. Be careful about the order in which you take your tricks. You may need to travel back and forth between your hand and the dummy. Play the high card from the short side first when taking tricks in a suit that's unevenly divided between the two hands. In a suit contract, play the trump first if you have all the tricks you need.

If you don't have enough tricks to make the contract, look for opportunities to get extra tricks through:

- Promoting winners from your high cards.
- Developing winners from your long suits.
- Leading toward a card you hope will win a trick.
- Using dummy's trumps to trump low cards from other suits.

Remember that this is a game with many challenging levels in both the bidding and the play. Start out by practicing the techniques from this book. Once you get more experience, pick up *Better Bridge—Play*, which is devoted to the play of the hand. There's a world of fascination at your fingertips.

Exercises

1. You reach a contract of 6NT, and the opening lead is the ♠J.

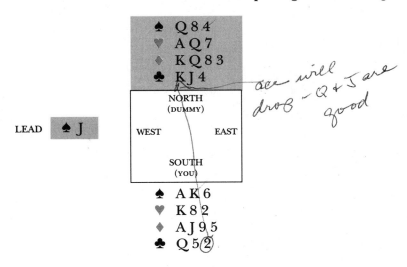

♠ Q 8 4
♥ A Q 7
♦ K Q 8 3
♣ K J 4

ace will drop — Q + J are good

NORTH
(DUMMY)

LEAD ♠ J

WEST   EAST

SOUTH
(YOU)

♠ A K 6
♥ K 8 2
♦ A J 9 5
♣ Q 5 2

a) How many tricks do you need to take? — *12*
b) How many sure tricks do you have? — *10*
c) Which suit do you plan to play after winning the first trick? *Clubs*
d) What technique will you use to make the contract?

low to high in dummy promotion

2. You reach a contract of 4♦ on the following hand, and the opening lead is the ♥J.

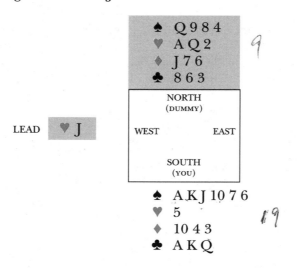

LEAD ♥ J

```
         ♠ Q 9 8 4
         ♥ A Q 2        9
         ♦ J 7 6
         ♣ 8 6 3
         NORTH
         (DUMMY)
    WEST          EAST

         SOUTH
         (YOU)
         ♠ A K J 10 7 6
         ♥ 5                 19
         ♦ 10 4 3
         ♣ A K Q
```

a) How many tricks do you need to take? ~ 10

b) How many sure tricks do you have? ~ 10

c) Will you play the ♥Q or ♥A from dummy on the first trick? AH

d) Which suit do you plan to play after winning a trick?

Answers to Exercises

1a) **Twelve**. A contract of 6NT requires 6 + 6 = 12 tricks.

1b) **Ten**. There are three sure spade tricks, three sure heart tricks, and four sure diamond tricks.

1c) **Clubs**. You need to develop two extra tricks from the club suit. You should plan to develop the club tricks while you still have high cards in all the other suits.

1d) **Promotion**. You need to drive out the defenders' ♣A, thereby promoting two winning tricks in the club suit.

2a) **Ten**. A contract of 4♠ requires 6 + 4 = 10 tricks.

2b) **Ten**. You have six sure spade tricks, the ♥A, and three top club tricks.

2c) **♥A**. You need ten tricks and can count ten tricks. There's no need to play the ♥Q on the first trick. East might hold the ♥K and win the trick. The defenders could then take three diamond tricks and defeat the contract. You have a sure thing. Don't drop the bone.

2d) **Spades**. After winning the first trick with the ♥A, draw the defenders' trumps by playing spades until the defenders have none left. It's then safe to take your club tricks. If you try to take the club tricks first, one of the defenders may be able to play a spade, trumping one of your sure tricks.

On the Defensive

"Come, Watson, come! The game is afoot."

—SIR ARTHUR CONAN DOYLE,
The Return of Sherlock Holmes

When you're defending a contract, bridge gives you a chance to play detective. The puzzle for the defenders is to figure out which suits to lead to defeat declarer's contract. There are clues to be found in the bidding and play of the hand. You'll need to interpret the evidence and use it to solve the puzzle.

The other side has outbid you during the auction, but you're going to have a second chance for success during the play. When the bidding took place, none of the players could see each other's cards. There's a chance that declarer's side has been overly ambitious during the auction. You'll have an opportunity to defeat the contract if you keep your ears and eyes open.

Starting Off

The defense makes the opening lead and puts the play of the hand in motion. When you're on lead, you have an important role to play for the partnership. You have to choose the suit to lead and the specific card within the suit to get the defense off on the right foot.

Choosing the Suit

In selecting the suit to lead, you need to look and listen for clues. "What clues?" you might be thinking. For one thing, you can see the thirteen cards in front of you. More important, you have had an opportunity to listen to the auction before choosing the opening lead. The sound of the auction will usually steer you in the right direction.

This is your hand:

         ♠ K 10 7 5 2
         ♥ 10 5 3
         ♦ Q J 6 4
         ♣ 8

You're sitting in the West position, and this is the auction you hear:

WEST (YOU)	NORTH	EAST (PARTNER)	SOUTH
	1♥	Pass	1♠
Pass	2♣	Pass	2NT
Pass	3NT	Pass	Pass
Pass			

When you're first learning the game, reading the auction can be a challenge. That's why I used those stuffed animals I mentioned way back in the first chapter. It helped me visualize how the written auction translates into what actually happened at the table. The player on your left, North, opens the bidding 1♥. Your partner passes, and the player on your right, South, responds 1♠. You pass, and the opening bidder on your left rebids 2♣. South rebids notrump, and North-South end up in a contract of 3NT.

You're to the left of South, the declarer, who first suggested notrump. So you must make the opening lead. You want to lead the suit that has the best potential for developing tricks for your side. Listen to what the opponents have told you through the auction.

They have hearts, spades, and clubs. Even without looking at your hand, it sounds as though diamonds would be a good choice for the defense. In an auction like this, diamonds are referred to as the *unbid suit*. With nothing much else to go on, it's a good idea to lead an unbid suit. Steer away from the suits the opponents seem to like.

Let's keep the same hand but change the auction:

WEST	NORTH	EAST	SOUTH
(YOU)		(PARTNER)	
	1♦	1♥	1NT
Pass	3NT	Pass	Pass
Pass			

This time the auction has given you a glimpse of partner's hand. Partner suggested hearts during the auction. It sounds like a good idea to lead partner's suit. That's probably where there's the most potential for tricks for your side.

Let's try an auction which provides you with very little information:

WEST	NORTH	EAST	SOUTH
(YOU)		(PARTNER)	
	Pass	Pass	1NT
Pass	3NT	Pass	Pass
Pass			

You aren't sure which suits the other three players have, so pick the suit that you like best. When defending a notrump contract, it's usually a good idea to choose your longest suit. You hope it will be the longest combined suit for the partnership and will provide the best source of tricks for your side. From the above hand, lead your longest suit, spades.

Finally, let's put you on lead against a suit contract, 4♥:

WEST	NORTH	EAST	SOUTH
(YOU)		(PARTNER)	
	1♠	Pass	2♥
Pass	3♥	Pass	4♥
Pass	Pass	Pass	

You could lead a diamond, one of the unbid suits, but you might also consider leading your singleton club. Hearts is the trump suit, and if partner can win the first trick and lead another club, you'll be able to trump the trick for your side—using the opponents' trump suit against them.

As you can see, you might lead any of the four suits from your hand. It all depends what hints you have from listening in on the bidding conversation.

Choosing the Card

Once you have decided on the suit to lead, the next decision is to select the specific card in the suit. As a defender, you're searching for clues, but at the same time, you want to provide clues to your partner. Hints are given through the specific cards you play to each trick.

Take out your deck of cards, and put the following hearts face up on the table:

♥ K Q J 10 7

Let's suppose you have decided to lead a heart, and these are the cards you hold in the suit. The defensive guideline when you have a sequence of touching cards headed by an honor is to lead the top of your touching cards. From this holding, you would lead the ♥K, top of the touching cards. To see why this is helpful to partner, turn all the other cards in the suit face down, and leave the ♥K face up on the table. Now, imagine that you're sitting in partner's position, on the other side of the table.

WEST (YOU)   EAST (PARTNER)
♥ K   ?

What conclusion can partner reach when you lead the ♥K? Since you lead the top of touching cards, partner can assume that you don't have the next higher card in the suit, the ♥A, but you do have the next lower card, the ♥Q, and perhaps the ♥J as well.

Replace the ♥K with the ♥Q face up on the table as the opening lead.

WEST (YOU)   EAST (PARTNER)
♥ Q   ?

What information will this card send to partner? Partner should know that you don't have the ♥K, the next higher card, but you do have the ♥J, and perhaps the ♥10 as well.

By leading the top of touching cards, you're telling partner three things. You like hearts, since you have chosen to lead the suit; you have the next lower card in the suit; you don't have the next higher card in the suit. Partner can play detective. If you lead the top of touching cards and your partner doesn't have the next higher card and dummy doesn't have it, it must be hidden in declarer's hand. All this from only one card.

Let's see how the partnership can work together to defeat a contract after leading the top card from a sequence. You're sitting in the East position. The player on your left opens the bidding 1NT, and the player on your right jumps to 3NT. Everyone passes, and it's your partner's lead. Partner leads the ♠K, and this is what you see when the dummy comes down:

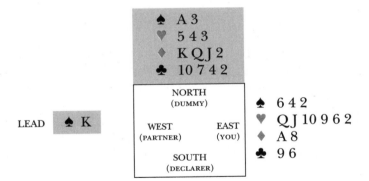

Partner's ♠K wins the first trick as declarer chooses to play the ♠3 from the dummy. Partner now leads the ♠5, and dummy wins the second trick with the ♠A. The ♦K is led from dummy, and you decide to win the trick with your ace. You have to decide what to lead next. The heart suit might look tempting. You have a sequence of your own and could lead the ♥Q, your top card. But—hold on a second.

The partnership is trying to take five tricks before declarer takes nine tricks. You don't know where the ♥A and ♥K are located, but you do know that partner has the ♠Q, and likely the ♠J as well— partner led the ♠K originally. Here's an important tip: lead back partner's suit unless you can clearly see a better alternative. Look what happens when you lead another spade:

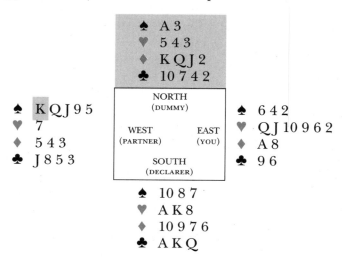

Your side ends up winning four spade tricks, together with your ♦A. That's enough to defeat the 3NT contract. If you lead back a heart, instead of a spade, declarer ends up taking a spade trick, two heart tricks, three diamond tricks, and three club tricks. Declarer would make the contract.

The defenders have to work together. They can't both be trying to establish their own suit. The opening lead has put the defense on the possible winning track. Switching tracks in mid-stream is rarely the best course.

The opening leader won't always have touching high cards from which to lead. Give yourself the following heart suit from which to lead:

♥ K J 8 4 3

If this is the suit you have chosen to lead, it's unlikely to do much good to lead the ♥K. You don't have the ♥Q to promote. Besides, if you lead the king, partner will expect that you also have the queen. When you don't have touching high cards, lead a low card.* The idea is that partner is going to have to come up with some help in this suit, perhaps the ♥A or ♥Q. You're leading over to partner's hoped-for high card, and partner can then lead the suit back to help the defense establish tricks. Let's see how that might work on the following hand where West has to lead against South's contract of 3NT.

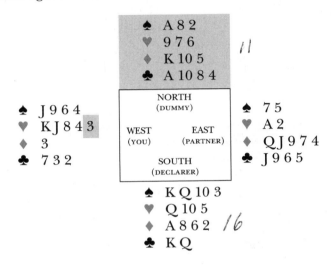

```
                     ♠ A 8 2
                     ♥ 9 7 6        //
                     ♦ K 10 5
                     ♣ A 10 8 4
                      NORTH
                     (DUMMY)
  ♠ J 9 6 4                              ♠ 7 5
  ♥ K J 8 4 3   WEST        EAST         ♥ A 2
  ♦ 3           (YOU)      (PARTNER)     ♦ Q J 9 7 4
  ♣ 7 3 2                                ♣ J 9 6 5
                      SOUTH
                    (DECLARER)
                     ♠ K Q 10 3
                     ♥ Q 10 5
                     ♦ A 8 6 2   /6
                     ♣ K Q
```

West starts off by leading a low heart—choosing to lead from the longest suit against the 3NT contract. When a low heart is played from dummy, East has to cooperate by playing third hand high and winning the trick with the ♥A. East still has more work to do. Leading a diamond might be tempting, but East should return partner's suit, leading back the ♥2. When South plays the ♥10, West can win the trick with the ♥J. West takes the next trick with the ♥K, removing the remaining hearts from declarer's and dummy's hand. West can now take two more heart tricks, defeating the 3NT contract.

The defenders take tricks using the same techniques for developing tricks as declarer. The last hand was actually an example of a finesse for the defense. When East led back a heart, South's ♥Q was trapped. South had to play before West chose a card. West was able

---

*Many players lead their fourth highest card in this situation, the ♥4. There are technical reasons for leading your fourth best card, but they're beyond the scope of this book. For now, lead your lowest card and it will work out fine.

to win tricks with both the ♥J and ♥K, even though the other partnership held the ♥Q. Do you remember the guideline for declarer about playing the high card from the short side first, so you don't need a taxi to get to the winners in the long hand? The defenders want to play their suits in the same way. Suppose your partner has bid hearts during the auction, but the opponents have arrived at a contract of 3NT. You have to make the opening lead from this hand:

♠ 10 7 5 4 3
♥ K 3
♦ 7 3 2
♣ 9 7 5

Although your longest suit is spades, you should lead the suit partner mentioned during the auction. You have a choice of leading the ♥K or the ♥3. When leading your own suit, lead the top of touching high cards, otherwise a low card. The situation here isn't the same. This time, it's your partner who has the length in the suit. You need to follow the same guideline as declarer. Lead the high card from the short side. Start with the ♥K. Here's the complete hand, with you in the West position:

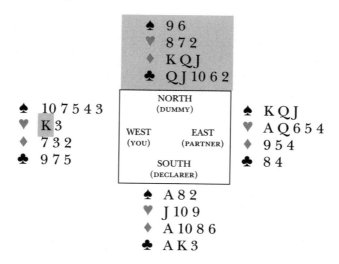

```
                    ♠ 9 6
                    ♥ 8 7 2
                    ♦ K Q J
                    ♣ Q J 10 6 2
                      NORTH
                     (DUMMY)
♠ 10 7 5 4 3                              ♠ K Q J
♥ K 3          WEST          EAST         ♥ A Q 6 5 4
♦ 7 3 2        (YOU)      (PARTNER)       ♦ 9 5 4
♣ 9 7 5                                   ♣ 8 4
                      SOUTH
                    (DECLARER)
                    ♠ A 8 2
                    ♥ J 10 9
                    ♦ A 10 8 6
                    ♣ A K 3
```

Your ♥K wins the first trick. Now you can lead the ♥3 as the taxi over to partner's ♥A. Partner can take the third trick with the ♥Q and then two more tricks in the heart suit because no one else has any left. The defense takes the first five tricks and defeats the contract.

Suppose you led the ♥3 to the first trick, and partner won the trick with the ♥A. Partner could lead another heart, and you would win the second trick with the ♥K. You have no hearts left. Whatever suit you lead, declarer can win and take one spade trick, four diamond tricks, and five club tricks—ten tricks. What a difference. The choice between two cards can mean the difference between success for the defenders or success for declarer. Notice, also, that if you led a spade originally, rather than partner's suit, declarer would be able to take the same ten tricks. Even the choice of suit to lead is critical on this hand. Did you think defending would be a boring part of the game?

Bridge is a partnership game. Be considerate of your partner. If your partner bids a suit, lead that suit. If partner leads a suit, return partner's suit if you get a chance later in the hand.

After the Opening Lead

The opening lead is made, the dummy comes down on the table, and now the declarer is trying to take enough tricks to make the contract. The defenders are also trying to take tricks. They're at a bit of a disadvantage, since they can't see the cards in each other's hand. It evens the playing field, however. There are advantages to being on defense. You have the opening lead, and you have to take fewer tricks to be successful. Having won the auction, declarer has to take at least seven tricks, and usually more, to make the contract. Besides, you have a partner.

As you have seen, the partnership starts exchanging information with the first card led, but there's more to it than that. Both defenders have to keep their eyes open for further clues.

Sending Signals

You aren't expected to be poker-faced throughout your bridge game. Once the hand is over, there's laughter, high spirits, and lots of stimulating conversation. Good table manners, however, dictate that when partner leads a suit you like, you avoid mouthing, "Yes!" You also can't suddenly take an interest in what's going on outside when partner leads a suit you don't like. The hints have to come from the cards you choose to play—not how you choose to play your cards. Here's how it works.

During the play, the defenders try to tell each other where tricks might come from through the use of signals. The cards themselves are used to show your attitude toward a particular suit. Suppose partner leads the ♦Q, and these are the diamonds you can see when the dummy comes down:

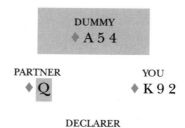

The lead of the ♦Q indicates that partner probably has the ♦J as well. Partner can see the ♦A in the dummy but doesn't know about the ♦K—it might be in your hand or in declarer's hand. Fortunately, you have a way of letting partner know.

Suppose the ♦A is played from the dummy. You now have a choice of cards to play. You don't want to play your king, and it may seem insignificant which of the other two cards you choose to play to the trick. This is a chance to send a signal. The standard agreement between defenders in this situation is that a high card says you like the suit and a low card says you don't like the suit. This is called an *attitude signal.* Holding the king, you're pleased about the suit partner has led, so you'd play the highest card you can afford, the ♦9. If you were to play the ♦2, your lowest card, you would be sending the message that you don't like the suit partner has chosen.

Suppose we change your holding in the diamond suit:

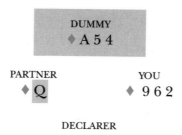

This time, you would play the ♦2, telling partner that you aren't particularly interested in this suit. Partner will probably draw the conclusion that you don't have the ♦K. This may help partner decide what to do later on in the defense of the hand.

Let's see how signaling can be put to use on a complete hand. You're sitting West with this hand:

♠ Q J 10 8
♥ A 3 2
♦ 9 6 5
♣ 9 7 5

The auction goes like this:

WEST	NORTH	EAST	SOUTH
(YOU)		(PARTNER)	
	1♦	Pass	1♥
Pass	2♦	Pass	4♥
Pass	Pass	Pass	

You have to make the opening lead against the contract of 4♥ and choose to lead the top of your touching cards in one of the unbid suits, the ♠Q. Dummy comes down, and this is what you see on the first trick:

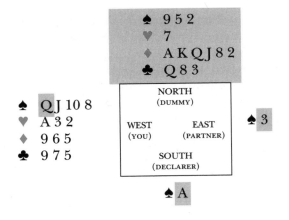

The ♠2 is played from dummy, partner plays the ♠3, and declarer wins the first trick with the ♠A. Declarer leads the ♥K, and you win the trick with the ♥A. Now what? If partner has the ♠K, your side may be able to take some spade tricks. If you were watching the card partner played on the first trick, however, you'll know that partner doesn't have the king. Partner played the ♠3 on the first trick. You could originally see the ♠2 in the dummy, so partner has sent you a discouraging signal in spades. It doesn't look as though leading a diamond or a trump is going to do much good. The only choice left is clubs. You lead a club, and this is the complete hand:

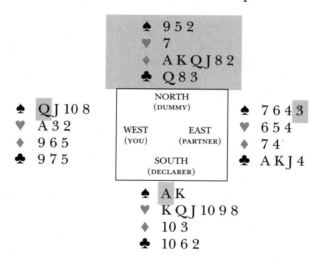

	NORTH (DUMMY)	
	♠ 9 5 2	
	♥ 7	
	♦ A K Q J 8 2	
	♣ Q 8 3	

WEST (YOU)		EAST (PARTNER)
♠ Q J 10 8		♠ 7 6 4 3
♥ A 3 2		♥ 6 5 4
♦ 9 6 5		♦ 7 4
♣ 9 7 5		♣ A K J 4

	SOUTH (DECLARER)	
	♠ A K	
	♥ K Q J 10 9 8	
	♦ 10 3	
	♣ 10 6 2	

Partner takes three club tricks because dummy's ♣Q is trapped, and the contract is defeated. If you'd led another spade, declarer would win the trick with the ♠K, draw the rest of the trump, and then take all the diamond tricks, discarding the clubs. Declarer would end up taking twelve tricks, rather than nine. Signals are very important to the defenders.

Making a Plan

The defenders, like the declarer, want to remind themselves of their objective. If the contract is 4♥, for example, the defenders have to take four tricks to be successful. Sometimes you'll need to visualize where your tricks might come from. Suppose partner leads the ♠J against a 4♥ contract, and this is what you see when the dummy is put down on the table:

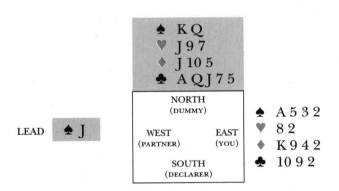

Your first thought might be to win the trick with the ♠A and return partner's suit. That's generally a good idea when you can see nothing better to do, but take a moment to formulate your plan. You need to take four tricks. Your side is going to get only one trick from the spade suit. It doesn't look as though you're going to take any tricks from the club suit. Even if partner has the ♣K, it's unlikely to do much good for the defense. The heart suit is the opponents' trump suit. Partner might have a trick or two in that suit, but that still doesn't give your side enough tricks to defeat the contract.

The only hope for the defense is in the diamond suit. You can't see through the backs of the cards, so you don't know what partner has in the diamond suit. That doesn't matter. You're trying to defeat the contract, and you're going to have to imagine something helpful in partner's hand in the diamond suit. This isn't the time to return partner's suit. Win the ♠A, and lead a diamond. Here's the complete hand:

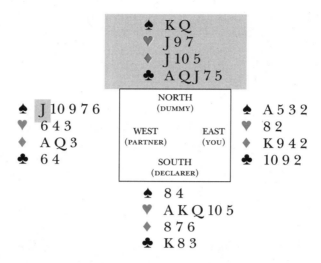

If you do anything but lead back a diamond at trick two, declarer will end up with eleven tricks—a spade trick, five heart tricks, and five club tricks. When you lead a diamond, the defense has a chance. Partner can win a trick with the ♦Q, and with the ♦A. That's three tricks for the defense. Now it's up to partner. Partner is going to have to hope that you have something useful in the diamond suit, and lead it again. If partner does anything else, declarer will take the rest of the tricks. Partner doesn't know for sure that you have the ♦K, but like you, partner is going to have to visualize a happy ending for the defense—and that's exactly what happens if partner leads another diamond.

Summary

The play of the hand starts with one defender making the opening lead. Listen to the bidding, and avoid leading one of the suits bid by the opponents during the auction. Choose an unbid suit or, if partner has bid during the auction, lead partner's suit. With no useful information, lead the suit you like best.

If you're leading against a notrump contract, you usually choose your longest suit. If you're leading against a suit contract, you sometimes lead a short suit—a singleton or a doubleton—hoping to make use of one of your trump cards before declarer draws the trumps.

Lead the top of touching high cards. Otherwise, lead low from a three-card or longer suit. If you're leading from a doubleton, lead the top card.

Signals can be given to your partner through the size of the cards that you play to a trick when you have a choice. A high card tends to be encouraging, asking partner to lead the suit. A low card tends to be discouraging, asking partner to look elsewhere for tricks.

Always keep in mind the goal of the defenders. Focus on how many tricks you need to take to defeat declarer's contract. Look at the sure tricks you have, and then look for ways to develop the extra tricks you need.

Exercises

1. The player on your right opens the bidding 1NT, and everyone passes. Which card do you lead from each of the following hands?

a) ♠ J 7 5
   ♥ Q J 10 8 7
   ♦ A 5 2
   ♣ 4 3

b) ♠ K 10 8 7 4
   ♥ A Q 3
   ♦ 6 2
   ♣ J 8 4

c) ♠ A K 5
   ♥ 6 2
   ♦ J 10 9 7 4
   ♣ J 6 3

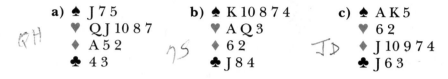

2. You have to make the opening lead with this hand:

♠ J 9 6 5 2
♥ 10 8 7 3
♦ J 3   — *top card from doubleton*
♣ A K

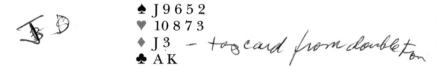

a) Which card would you lead if the opponents are in 3NT, and partner bid diamonds during the auction?

b) Which card would you lead if the opponents are in 3NT, and nobody bid a suit during the auction?

c) Which card would you lead if the opponents are in a contract of 6NT?

3. Partner's opening lead is the ♣3 against the opponent's 4♥ contract, and dummy's ♣A is played to the first trick. Which club do you play in each of the following situations?

a)

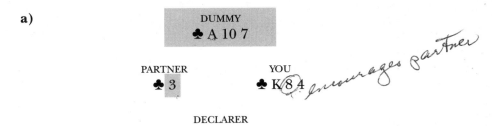

	DUMMY	
	♣ A 10 7	
PARTNER		YOU
♣ 3		♣ K 8 4
	DECLARER	

encourages partner

b)

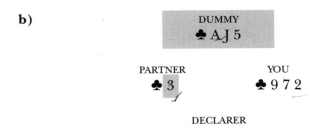

	DUMMY	
	♣ A J 5	
PARTNER		YOU
♣ 3		♣ 9 7 2
	DECLARER	

Answers to Exercises

1a) ♥Q. Choose your longest suit. Lead the top of your touching high cards.

1b) ♠4 (or ♠7). Choose your longest suit. With no touching high cards, lead a low card.

1c) ♦J. Even though your ♠A and ♠K are sure tricks, you want to establish tricks from your long suit. Start by leading the top of the touching cards in your longest suit.

2a) ♦J. Lead partner's suit. Lead the top card from a doubleton.

2b) ♠2 (or ♠5). With nothing to go on, choose your longest suit. Lead a low card when you don't have touching high cards.

2c) ♣A. Always keep your objective in mind. You need only two tricks to defeat the 6NT contract. Lead your ♣A and then the ♣K. Partner will certainly be pleased.

3a) ♣8. You like partner's choice of suit, since you have the king. Give partner an encouraging signal by playing the highest card you can afford.

3b) ♣2. This time, partner's choice of suit doesn't look so great. Play your lowest club, sending a discouraging signal. This tells partner to look elsewhere for help from your hand.

Everyone Can Play

"Much might be said on both sides."
—JOSEPH ADDISON,
The Spectator [July 20, 1711]

Remember the very first hand we watched in the lobby of Brown's Hotel? That seems like a long time ago. The players from both sides were bidding during the auction, and that's a common occurrence. When both partnerships are bidding, it's referred to as a *competitive auction* or bidding with *competition*. So far, we've discussed only how one partnership bids back and forth to try to reach a reasonable contract. It's time to let everyone in on the action.

Getting into the Auction

Only one player can open the bidding. That's the first player to say something other than pass. After that, either side can make the next bid. In a competitive auction, there are two quite different ways to enter into the auction. Let's look at them both.

Overcalls

At the hotel, we were watching over South's shoulder during the auction, but let's suppose we were sitting behind East. The auction started like this:

WEST	NORTH	EAST	SOUTH
	1♣	?	

Here's East's hand:

♠ 7
♥ K Q J 8 7
♦ Q 5 3
♣ K J 10 6

North opened the bidding 1♣, and East was next to speak. East has enough strength to open the bidding, but it has already been opened. Still, there's nothing to stop East from competing for the contract, and with this hand, East bid 1♥. This bid is called an *overcall* because it's a call over the opponent's bid.

Overcalls have a lot in common with opening bids. You're committing the partnership to take at least seven tricks and you're suggesting a trump suit. Ideally, you would like to have at least as much strength as the opening bidder when you make an overcall—13 or more points. In practice, you often have less because it's a good strategy to get into the auction whenever possible. Your side might win the auction, you could interfere with the other side's bidding, and you might help partner find a good opening lead if your side ends up defending. The most important requirement for an overcall is that you have a good suit, usually five or more cards in length. One reason for having a good suit to make an overcall is that partner will tend to lead your suit if the other side wins the auction. Your overcall has given partner a clue about your length and strength.

For example, suppose you're sitting West, and the auction goes like this:

WEST	NORTH	EAST	SOUTH
(YOU)		(PARTNER)	
	1♦	Pass	1NT
Pass	3NT	Pass	Pass
Pass			

You have to make the opening lead from this hand:

♠ 4 2
♥ Q J 10 5 4
♦ 7 3
♣ J 10 9 3

You would probably select the ♥Q, top of the touching cards in your longest suit. With nothing else to go on, you're hoping that partner has some help in the heart suit and that your side can develop enough tricks from the suit to defeat the contract. Now, let's change the auction slightly:

WEST	NORTH	EAST	SOUTH
(YOU)		(PARTNER)	
	1♦	1♠	1NT
Pass	3NT	Pass	Pass
Pass			

Your partner has made an overcall, suggesting spades as the trump suit. You haven't been able to win the auction, but partner's bid has given you a clue about what to lead. Accepting partner's suggestion, you lead the ♠4, top of your doubleton. Here's the complete hand:

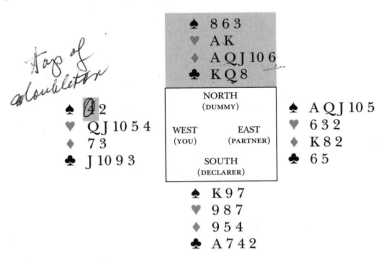

top of doubleton

```
                    ♠ 8 6 3
                    ♥ A K
                    ♦ A Q J 10 6
                    ♣ K Q 8
                      NORTH
                     (DUMMY)
♠ 4 2          WEST          EAST      ♠ A Q J 10 5
♥ Q J 10 5 4   (YOU)      (PARTNER)    ♥ 6 3 2
♦ 7 3                                  ♦ K 8 2
♣ J 10 9 3           SOUTH             ♣ 6 5
                   (DECLARER)
                    ♠ K 9 7
                    ♥ 9 8 7
                    ♦ 9 5 4
                    ♣ A 7 4 2
```

After your spade lead, partner wins the first trick with the ♠A, and then leads the ♠Q. After winning a trick with the ♠K, declarer has only six more sure tricks: the ♥A and ♥K, the ♦A, and the ♣A, ♣K, and ♣Q. That's not enough to make the contract. Sooner or later, declarer will have to try to get extra tricks from the diamond suit. Your partner can win a trick with the ♦K and take the rest of the spade tricks. The defense will end up with four spade tricks and a diamond trick, enough to defeat the contract of 3NT.

Partner has only 10 high card points plus 1 point for the five-card suit. That's not enough to open the bidding, but it was a good decision to make an overcall. Without that information, you would lead a heart, and declarer would make the contract. Declarer would be able to take four diamond tricks by driving out partner's ♦K and would also have two heart tricks and three club tricks. It's too late for the defense to lead spades after winning a trick with the ♦K. South still has the ♠K left to win the second round of the suit.

Another advantage of the overcall is that it can interfere with the smooth flow of the other partnership's auction. Suppose your partner is North, and opens the bidding 1♦. You're sitting South, planning to make your response with this hand:

♠ K 9 7 3
♥ K J 9 5
♦ 9 5
♣ K 4 2

If East, on your right, says pass, you can respond 1♥ with this hand, looking for a major suit fit. Suppose, however, there's an overcall of 1♠ on your right. You have only 10 points, not enough to go to the two level to introduce a new suit. Instead, you might compromise by responding 1NT, showing 6–10 points. Everyone passes. Here's the auction and the complete hand:

WEST	NORTH	EAST	SOUTH
	(PARTNER)		(YOU)
	1♦	1♠	1NT
Pass	Pass	Pass	

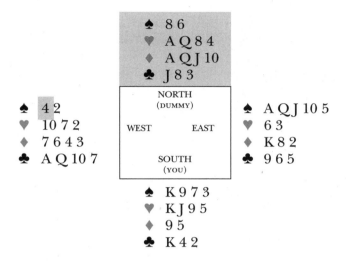

♠ 8 6
♥ A Q 8 4
♦ A Q J 10
♣ J 8 3

NORTH
(DUMMY)

♠ 4 2
♥ 10 7 2
♦ 7 6 4 3
♣ A Q 10 7

WEST   EAST

♠ A Q J 10 5
♥ 6 3
♦ K 8 2
♣ 9 6 5

SOUTH
(YOU)

♠ K 9 7 3
♥ K J 9 5
♦ 9 5
♣ K 4 2

West leads the ♣4, and East wins the trick with the ♣A. East leads back the ♣Q, and you win the trick with the ♣K. You can take four heart tricks, and the ♦A, but that's only six tricks. If you try to establish your seventh trick in diamonds, East wins a trick with the ♦K, takes three more spade tricks, and leads a club. West gets two club tricks, and again you end up with only six tricks. You can't make your contract of 1NT.

If East hadn't overcalled, you would have been able to show your heart suit at the one level. Partner would have supported your hearts, and you would have reached a partscore of 2♥. Playing in your eight-card trump fit, you would be able to take eight tricks, making your contract—four heart tricks, three diamond tricks, and the ♣K. Quite a difference.

The simple overcall of 1♠ interfered with your auction, and you landed in the wrong contract. That will often happen in competitive auctions. There's not always enough room left to search for the best spot. Having both sides bidding at the same time introduces a new level of challenge to the game.

Responding to an Overcall

If partner makes an overcall, treat it in a similar fashion to an opening bid. Partner may have less than the strength required for an opening bid, but there's compensation in the fact that partner has a good five-card suit or longer. You can show support for partner's suit if you have three or more cards. Otherwise, you can bid a suit of your own or bid notrump. You still need six or more points to bid at the one level and eleven or more to introduce a new suit at the two level.

Here are some examples. North is the dealer, you're West, and the auction starts off:

WEST	NORTH	EAST	SOUTH
(YOU)		(PARTNER)	
	1♣	1♥	1♠
?			

♠ A 4
♥ J 10 5
♦ Q J 9 4
♣ 8 6 4 2

Bid 2♥. Your hand falls into the 6–10 point category, about right for a raise to the two level. Partner should have a five-card or longer suit, so there's an eight-card fit. You may not end up winning the auction, but you do want to compete for the contract. You would rather have hearts as the trump suit than let the other side choose the trump suit.

♠ A 4
♥ K J 10 5
♦ Q J 9 4
♣ 8 6 4

Bid 3♥. The jump raise shows about 11–12 points. It won't matter if partner has only 9 or 10 points for the overcall. If your side is too high, the opponents could probably make a contract of their own. In competitive auctions, it's often difficult to tell which side should win the auction.

♠ A 4
♥ 10 5
♦ K Q J 9 4 2
♣ 6 4 2

Bid 2♦. With 10 high card points plus 2 points for the six-card suit, you have enough to introduce a suit of your own, even though it has to be bid at the two level. Sounds like everyone has a suit they want to introduce in this auction.

♠ 7 4
♥ J 10 5
♦ Q J 9 4
♣ 8 6 4 2

Pass. With fewer than 6 points, you can keep quiet. You can't afford to get too high on the bidding ladder. In a competitive auction, partner will get another opportunity to say something with a very strong hand.

Takeout Doubles

There's another way to come into the auction other than by making an overcall. You can make special use of a bid we haven't talked about much up to this point—the double.

The double is sometimes used toward the end of the auction when you don't think the other side can make their contract. This is a *penalty double,* and it increases the score if the contract is made or if it's defeated. During the early stages of the auction, however, the double can be put to a more useful purpose.

The double can be a three-for-one sale. That's right, one word to show a hand with interest in three suits. Suppose you're sitting East with the following hand, and the player on your right opens the bidding with 1♥:

♠ A 8 4 3
♥ 7
♦ K Q J 3
♣ K 10 9 3

You have an interest in having any suit as trump—except the one mentioned by your opponent. You also have a hand of better than average strength, with the values for an opening bid. To send the message to partner that you would like to compete in the auction with this hand, you say "double," rather than making an overcall.

WEST	NORTH	EAST	SOUTH
(PARTNER)		(YOU)	
	1♥	Double	

The double in this situation says, "Bid your best suit, partner—I have support for any of the unbid suits and would like to compete for the contract." This bid is referred to as a *takeout double* because you're asking partner to take you out of the double and bid a suit. Partner isn't expected to pass, even with a weak hand. To make a takeout double, there are several things you should know.

What's the first letter in the word double? Right, a "D." There's another word that starts with "D" and that's "Dummy." The takeout doubler counts dummy points when valuing the hand. A void is worth 5 points; a singleton, 3 points; a doubleton, 1 point. The double asks partner to pick the suit, and so the doubler is going to be putting down the hand as the dummy. You need about the values for an opening bid in order to make a takeout double. The above hand would be worth 16 points—13 high card points plus 3 dummy points. That's more than enough. Look at this hand:

♠ K 10 9 3
♥ 7
♦ A J 10 5
♣ Q 10 8 6

Although there are only 10 high card points, this hand is worth 13 points when you include 3 dummy points for the singleton heart. If the player on your right opens the bidding 1♥, you could make a takeout double with this hand. When you do this, some onlookers may praise your card sense and give you credit for knowing how to value the hand. Others might think you're lucky—finding a successful way to enter the auction with only 10 high card points. In fact, you're following the standard practice by counting dummy points when thinking about making a takeout double.

The word "unbid" is also important. A takeout double shows support for the unbid suits—those not bid by the opponents. Consider this hand:

♠ 8 7
♥ Q J 9 8 4
♦ A J 3
♣ K Q 4

If the opening bid on your right is 1♥, what are you going to say? You can't use the takeout double. Although you have the values for an opening bid, the double would show support for the unbid suits.

You wouldn't be too happy if partner chose spades as the trump suit. The hand isn't suitable for an overcall either. The only long suit you have is hearts, the suit bid by your opponent. It's not a good idea to suggest that suit as trump. The opponent on your right has contracted to take seven tricks with hearts as trump—it's not too likely that you can take eight tricks in the same trump suit.

This is the time to stay quiet and pass. You don't have to bid when you have thirteen or more points, and the other side has opened the bidding. If your hand isn't suitable for either an overcall or a takeout double, you should pass. You can still have some fun with this kind of hand. See what happens next. You may get to use the double in another context—which brings us to the penalty double.

There are two different meanings that can be assigned to the bid of double. It can ask partner to pick a suit; this is a takeout double. It can also be used to suggest that the opponents have bid too much; this is the penalty double. How does partner know when the double is meant for takeout and when it's meant for penalty? One guideline is that a double at the partscore level is for takeout provided it's made at your first opportunity and partner hasn't already made a bid other than pass. Otherwise, it's a penalty double.

If you were to pass with the above hand and wait until the other side reached 4♥ before saying double, that would be for penalty. You're no longer at the partscore level, and you didn't make a takeout double when you had the opportunity. If partner opened the bidding 1♠, and the player on your right overcalled 2♥, you could make a penalty double. There's no need to use a takeout double to ask partner to pick a suit because you already know which suit partner prefers.

Using the takeout double takes a little practice, but you'll soon find it's a very useful way to get into the auction when you don't have one good suit to show with an overcall. The logic of the auction will usually indicate whether a double is for penalty or for takeout.

Responding to a Takeout Double

The most important thing to remember about responding to a takeout double is that you have to make a bid if the player on your right says pass. Suppose you're sitting West, and the auction starts this way:

WEST	NORTH	EAST	SOUTH
(YOU)		(PARTNER)	
	1♥	Double	Pass
?			

You're holding this hand:

♠ Q 8 6 2
♥ J 6 3
♦ 9 5
♣ J 10 6 4

You have only 4 points. If partner had opened the bidding, you would pass. An opening bid at the one level is an invitational bid, and you usually pass with fewer than 6 points. The takeout double, however, is a forcing bid. Partner has asked you to pick the trump suit. Your best suit is spades, so you should respond 1♠, showing your suit at the cheapest available level, since you don't have any extra strength.

Responses to a takeout double follow a familiar pattern: the more you have the more you bid. With 10 or fewer points, bid at the cheapest possible level; with a medium-strength hand about 11–12 points, jump a level to show invitational strength; and with 13 or more points take the partnership to the game level.

Here are some examples. You're sitting West, and North begins the auction.

WEST	NORTH	EAST	SOUTH
(YOU)		(PARTNER)	
	1♠	Double	Pass
?			

♠ J 9 5
♥ 10 2
♦ K 8 4
♣ Q 9 7 6 3

Respond 2♣. Partner has asked you to choose the trump suit. With 0–10 points, you show your suit at the cheapest available level. With this hand, you have to go to the two level. This isn't quite the same as responding to an opening bid where you need 11 or more points to bid a new suit at the two level. Partner has forced you to bid. It's similar to raising one of partner's suits.

♠ J 5   Jump to 3♥. Partner's takeout double shows
♥ K J 9 7 2   the values for an opening bid and support for
♦ A 9 8   all the unbid suits, including hearts. With a
♣ Q 9 7   hand in the 11–12 point range, the partnership must be close to the combined strength
for a game contract. You would respond at the cheapest available
level, 2♥, with a minimum hand. So, you should jump a level to
invite partner to carry on to game with a little extra. Partner can still
pass and leave the partnership in partscore with only 13 or 14 points.

♠ J 5   *14♣*   Bid 4♥. You have the values for an opening
♥ A J 10 7 2.   bid, and partner is showing the values for an
♦ A 9 4   opening bid. The partnership should have at
♣ K 9 7   least 26 combined points. Bid to the game
level in your eight-card or longer trump fit.
You know partner has three or four hearts, since the takeout double
shows support for the unbid suits.

Competitive Auctions

In competitive auctions there's not usually enough room in the auction for everyone to describe their hand perfectly. You'll have to
make compromises and do the best you can. That's part of the game.
You're trying to reach your best contract, and at the same time, prevent the other side from reaching its best contract—especially when
the strength is evenly divided between the two partnerships.

Silence Can Be Golden

When partner opens the bidding and the other side enters the auction, it may or may not affect your response. If the opponent on your
right makes a takeout double, no bidding room has been taken up,
and you can bid on as though the opponents aren't even there. After
an overcall, things may be a little different. Let's consider some sample
hands when you're sitting South, and the auction starts this way:

	WEST	NORTH	EAST	SOUTH
		(PARTNER)		(YOU)
		1♥	2♦	?

♠ K 5 2
♥ Q 10 7 4
♦ 8 4
♣ Q 6 4 2

2♥. No problem. You were planning to raise partner's suit to the two level, and East's bid didn't get in your way.

♠ K Q 8 6 4
♥ 7 4
♦ 9 8 4
♣ Q J 5

Pass. This time East's bid has presented you with a challenge. You would have responded 1♠ if East had passed, since you can show a new suit at the one level with 6 or more points. You aren't strong enough to introduce the spade suit after the overcall. You'd have to bid 2♠, and a new suit at the two level requires about 11 or more points. Instead, pass for now. Once East bids, partner will get another opportunity in the auction. With a strong hand, partner can bid again when the auction comes back around. You may get a chance to show your spade suit later.

♠ A K J 9 7 5
♥ 6 2
♦ 9 3
♣ K 8 4

2♠. Without the overcall, you would respond 1♠, showing your suit at the most convenient level. The overcall forces a change in plan. With 11 high card points plus 2 for the six-card suit, you have enough to bid your suit at the two level. No real problem. You're heading for the game level anyway, once partner opens the bidding.

♠ K 10 3
♥ J 5
♦ Q 7 6 2
♣ J 9 6 4

Pass. You planned to respond 1NT, showing 6–10 points with no suit to bid at the one level. The overcall has taken away that opportunity. You can't afford to bid 2NT. That shows about 11–12 points and invites partner to continue to game with only a little extra. The partnership might be too high. Silence is best. The auction isn't over yet, and even if everyone passes, it may be fun defending with diamonds as trump.

♠ A J 3   Double. You were planning to respond 2♦,
♥ 6   and East got there first. The overcall does
♦ A Q 10 9 5   make another bid available, the penalty
♣ J 10 6 2   double. This isn't a takeout double because
                 partner has already bid. The penalty double
says you don't think the other side can make their contract—and
that's probably the case when you hold this hand. Unlucky for East.

Play or Defend?

When both sides are bidding, you'll often be faced with the decision
of whether to bid more so that your side can play the contract or to
pass and defend, letting the opponents choose the trump suit. The
decision is always a challenge. For example, suppose you're sitting
South with this hand:

♠ J 4
♥ K 10 8 3   *9*
♦ A J 6 2
♣ 10 8 5

Partner opens the bidding 1♥, and the auction starts off this way:

WEST	NORTH	EAST	SOUTH
	(PARTNER)		(YOU)
	1♥	1♠	2♥
2♠	Pass	Pass	?

East's overcall doesn't give you any difficulty. You raise to 2♥ showing your support for partner's suit and about 6–10 points. It would
be nice if the auction finished at this point with everyone saying
pass. Partner could play in a partscore contract of 2♥ and try to take
eight tricks. West, however, isn't going to let you get away that easily.
West competes to 2♠, showing support for East's trump suit. Your
partner has a minimum-strength hand and can't afford to bid any
higher. The auction comes back to you.

You have a decision to make. Do you pass and let the other side
buy the contract with their suit as trumps, or do you bid 3♥? Partner
will have to take nine tricks if you bid, but at least your side will be

playing with hearts as the trump suit. There's no right answer—that's what makes the game such great entertainment. Do what you think is best, and see how it turns out. If your choice doesn't work out well, there's always the next hand.

Summary

There are many auctions where both sides are competing for the contract. If your opponents have opened the bidding, you have two ways to compete. You make an overcall, showing a good five-card or longer suit; or you can make a takeout double, showing the values for an opening bid and asking partner to choose one of the unbid suits as trump.

An overcall by partner is an invitational bid, and you respond in a similar fashion to responding to an opening bid. A takeout double by partner is a forcing bid, and unless the player on your right makes a bid, you're expected to bid your best suit. With 0–10 points, bid at the cheapest available level. With 11–12 points, jump a level of bidding. With 13 or more points, take the partnership to the game level. The more you have, the more you bid.

In competitive auctions, you may not be able to make the bid you would like. Do the best you can. You don't have to bid if you have nothing convenient to say, but you also don't want to let the other side buy the contract too cheaply. Take some chances and have fun.

Exercises

1. The player on your right opens the bidding 1♦. What would you do with each of the following hands? *13*

14

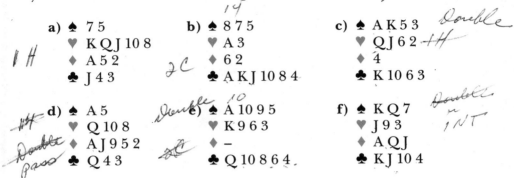

1 H

a) ♠ 7 5
   ♥ K Q J 10 8
   ♦ A 5 2
   ♣ J 4 3

b) ♠ 8 7 5
   ♥ A 3
   ♦ 6 2
   ♣ A K J 10 8 4   *2 C*

c) ♠ A K 5 3   *Double*
   ♥ Q J 6 2   *1H*
   ♦ 4
   ♣ K 10 6 3

1H
Double
pass

d) ♠ A 5
   ♥ Q 10 8
   ♦ A J 9 5 2
   ♣ Q 4 3

Double
e) ♠ A 10 9 5   *10*
   ♥ K 9 6 3
   ♦ –
   ♣ Q 10 8 6 4   *2C*

f) ♠ K Q 7   *Double*
   ♥ J 9 3   *n*
   ♦ A Q J   *1 NT*
   ♣ K J 10 4

2. What would you bid as South with each of the following hands after the auction starts off:

WEST	NORTH (PARTNER)	EAST	SOUTH (YOU)
1♦	1♠	2♦	?

8   *10+1*   *14+3*

2S

a) ♠ K 7 5
   ♥ A 10 8
   ♦ J 5 2
   ♣ 10 9 4 2

b) ♠ K J 6 3
   ♥ K Q 8 5
   ♦ J 10 2
   ♣ 8 4   *3S*

11–12 pts

c) ♠ J 9 7 6
   ♥ A 9 6
   ♦ 5
   ♣ K Q 10 6 3   *4S*

3. What would you bid as South with each of the following hands after the auction starts off:

WEST	NORTH (PARTNER)	EAST	SOUTH (YOU)
1♦	Double	Pass	?

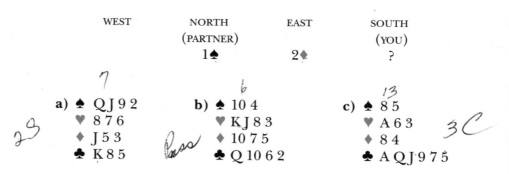

(handwritten: 3)

a) ♠ 10 9 6 3
♥ J 8
♦ Q 6 4 3
♣ 10 8 7

(handwritten: 1S)

(handwritten: 11)

b) ♠ K 7 6
♥ K Q 8 5 2
♦ Q 8 6
♣ 10 4

(handwritten: 2H)

(handwritten: 12 + 1)

c) ♠ A J 10 7 5
♥ 6 3
♦ K 8 4
♣ K J 7

(handwritten: 4S)

4. What would you bid as South with each of the following hands after the auction starts off:

WEST	NORTH (PARTNER)	EAST	SOUTH (YOU)
	1♠	2♦	?

(handwritten: 7)

a) ♠ Q J 9 2
♥ 8 7 6
♦ J 5 3
♣ K 8 5

(handwritten: 2S)

(handwritten: 6)

b) ♠ 10 4
♥ K J 8 3
♦ 10 7 5
♣ Q 10 6 2

(handwritten: Pass)

(handwritten: 13)

c) ♠ 8 5
♥ A 6 3
♦ 8 4
♣ A Q J 9 7 5

(handwritten: 3C)

Answers to Exercises

1a) **1♥**. Although you have only 11 high card points plus 1 point for the fifth heart, you have a good suit for an overcall.

1b) **2♣**. This is a good hand for an overcall, even though you have to start the bidding for your side at the two level.

1c) **Double**. You have the values for an opening bid and support for all the unbid suits. Make a takeout double, and ask partner to choose the trump suit.

1d) **Pass**. Although you would have opened the bidding 1♦, the player on your right has bid your suit first. You don't have the right hand for an overcall or a takeout double. Pass and await developments.

1e) **Double**. Although there are only 9 high card points, you can value your hand using dummy points when considering a takeout double. Count 5 dummy points for the diamond void, and your hand is strong enough to enter the auction. Giving partner a choice of three suits is better than overcalling your weak five-card club suit at the two level.

1f) **1NT**. An overcall of 1NT shows the same type of hand as an opening bid of 1NT.

2a) **2♠**. With 8 points, you have enough to raise partner's overcall to the two level and compete for the contract.

2b) **3♠**. You have 10 high card points plus 1 dummy point for the doubleton club. Raise partner's suit to the three level, showing your support and about 11–12 points.

2c) **4♠**. You have 10 high card points and can add 3 dummy points for the singleton. That's enough to take partner to the game level.

3a) **1♠**. Partner's takeout double has asked you to pick a trump suit other than the suit bid by the opponents. With only 3 points, bid your suit at the cheapest available level.

3b) **2♥**. You can count 10 high card points plus 1 point for the five-card suit. Jump a level of bidding to invite partner to carry on to game with a little extra for the takeout double.

3c) **4♠**. Your hand is worth an opening bid, and partner has shown the values for an opening bid. The partnership should have 26 or more combined points. Bid to the game level in your suit. Partner has promised support.

4a) **2♠**. The overcall doesn't prevent you from showing support for partner's suit and a hand worth 6–10 points. Raise to the two level.

4b) **Pass**. You would have responded 1NT if East hadn't overcalled. With only 6 points, you don't have enough to bid a new suit at the two level or to bid 2NT. Pass for now.

4c) **3♣**. You would have responded 2♣, a new suit at the two level, if there had been no overcall. Now you'll have to show your suit at the three level. That should be fine. The partnership should have enough combined strength to reach the game level.

Where Next?

"The play's the thing . . ."

—WILLIAM SHAKESPEARE,
Hamlet

You now know enough, having read to this point in the book, to play in a bridge game. Let's look at some of the things that will help you get off to a good start.

Where Do I Find a Bridge Game?

Bridge games are found everywhere; they're in clubs, condominiums, libraries, community centers, churches, synagogues, private homes, parks—the possibilities are endless. Bridge is a game played all over the world.

When you're starting out, you want to look for a friendly game that isn't too far beyond your current level. You might have friends or family who play bridge, and that's probably a good place to start. Almost every small town has a local bridge club. You need to be a little careful jumping into these games because some of the players may have been playing for a number of years. You may, however, be able to inquire from your local club where there are games more suitable to the level at which you want to play.

If there isn't a game in your community, you might be the person to get one started. For example, you could ask the librarian, or the program director at your work or school, to help organize a bridge group. Put an announcement up on a bulletin board, stating a time and place for casual bridge players to meet.

Finding Partners

Using the guidelines in this book, you can play with anyone as your partner. As you get more familiar with the game, you might want to develop regular partnerships with two or three other bridge players. That way, you can discuss your bidding, play, and defense and move forward, learning new things about the game together. It helps to have a partner who plays the same style as you do.

Improving Your Game

The wonderful thing about bridge is that it's an ongoing learning process. You may be happy playing the occasional game of bridge, or you may want to learn more. If you're interested in learning more, there are lots of possibilities.

Books on Bridge

There are hundreds of books that have been written about the game. When choosing a book, make sure it's suitable to your level. Most books assume you already know a great deal about the game, and you may soon be beyond your depth.

There are three more books in this series. *Better Bridge—Bidding* is a good choice if you want to expand this part of your game. *Better Bridge—Play* covers the play of the hand in more detail, and *Better Bridge—Defense* will improve your skills in that area. Pass the books around. Get a set for the library at your work. Put them out on the lunch room table. It's helpful if the people you play with use similar methods and have the same outlook on the game.

Bridge Lessons

Most communities offer bridge lessons. These are a good way to meet people with similar interests. Be sure both the teacher and the curriculum are suitable.

Some bridge teachers and bridge clubs run supervised games. These allow you to ask for help during the bidding and play and include a discussion at the end of each hand. They can be a good way to practice what you've learned.

Would You Play Bridge with Us?

"Would you like to join us for a game of bridge?" comes the question. "We need a fourth." Whether this happens while you're on vacation, at work, with your family and friends, or with some acquaintances, it might bring the odd butterfly to your stomach.

Here are a few hints. First, briefly inform the other players that you're learning the game. If they're willing to accept this, you're playing bridge. One sentence is enough about your level of experience. There's no need, during the bidding or play, to emphasize your lack of experience by saying such things as, "I don't know how to sort the cards...or what to bid...or what to lead. Excuse me for a moment while I run home to get my book." Probably the phrase "silence is golden" is one to consider when you're gaining experience. For example, if you end up playing the contract and make 3NT, there's no need to comment on how truly surprised you are that you took nine tricks. If you put the ♣2 on the table and it wins the trick, try to avoid a look of astonishment.

Your partner may ask you a question like this, "Do you play the Stayman Convention?" You might answer, with a pleasant smile, "No, but thanks for asking." Then add, gently and without sarcasm, "I think it would be best for our partnership to avoid any conventions, even Stayman. I'm sure with your experience, you'll welcome the chance to get to the best level and denomination without conventions."

It's unlikely, but you might find after sitting down to play that one of the players at the table becomes critical of your bidding or play. You should, without fuss, leave the game as soon as possible. You need to find a new group of bridge players.

Focus on the Concepts

You know enough to play a pleasant game of bridge. You know that the dealer distributes all the cards and that your bridge hand will have 13 cards. The dealer has the first chance to either pass or bid a suit. When it's your turn to call, you open at the one level with a minimum of 13 points. You might have a balanced hand with 16, 17, or 18 points and be able to start the bidding with 1NT. If you don't have the qualifications for an opening bid of 1NT, you could start with an opening bid of one-in-a-suit.

Keep the big picture in focus. The bidding is a conversation among the players to decide on the trump suit or notrump. Your goal is to try to get to one of the game bonus levels. Favor 3NT, 4♥, and 4♠. On rare occasions, you might be headed for one of the slam bonuses.

When playing the hand, stop for a moment before you play a card to the first trick. Think about how many tricks you need, how many you have, and how you might get the extra ones you need.

When defending, keep your eyes and ears open. Listen to the bidding and watch the cards that are being played, even the little ones. Partner's cards might be sending you a message.

A Closing Comment

I hope you've enjoyed reading the book and that the game of bridge brings you many happy hours of entertainment. I look forward to seeing you some day at the bridge table.

Glossary

attitude signal The play of a specific card to a trick to inform partner whether or not you like a particular suit. A high card is usually encouraging, a low card discouraging.

auction The bidding by the four players to decide on the contract.

balanced hand A hand containing no voids, no singletons, and at most one doubleton. There are three balanced hand patterns: 4-3-3-3, 4-4-3-2, and 5-3-3-2.

bid A commitment made during the auction for the partnership to take at least a declared number of tricks with the hand played in a specific trump suit or notrump.

bonus points Points, other than the trick score, awarded for bidding and making contracts. The bonuses depend on the form of scoring.

call A bid, double, redouble, or pass made during the auction.

certain trick A trick which can be taken without giving up the lead to the opponents. Same as sure trick.

competition When both partnerships are bidding for the contract.

competitive auction An auction in which both partnerships are bidding.

contract The final bid identifying the number of tricks to be taken in the specified denomination by the partnership winning the auction.

cut Divide the deck into two approximately equal parts and place the bottom half on the top. Also refers to randomly drawing a card from a face down deck.

deal The distribution of the cards in the deck to the four players. The cards are distributed face down in a clockwise direction.

deck The fifty-two cards used in a game of bridge. It contains four suits, with thirteen cards in each suit.

declarer The player from the partnership winning the auction who first mentioned the denomination of the final contract. Declarer selects the cards from both the partnership hands during the play.

defeat   Take enough tricks as defenders to prevent declarer from fulfilling the contract.

defenders   The members of the partnership that did not win the auction. They try to defeat the contract.

denomination   The suit or notrump named in a bid.

directions   The four players in a bridge game are often referred to using the points on a compass: North, East, South, and West. North and South are partners; East and West are partners.

discard   Contribute a card to a trick which is neither from the suit led nor from the trump suit.

doubleton   A holding of two cards in a suit.

drawing trump   Playing the trump suit to remove the trump cards held by the opponents.

dummy   The cards held by declarer's partner. They are placed face up on the table after the opening lead.

dummy points   Points used in place of length points when valuing a hand in support of partner's suit: void, 5 points; singleton, 3 points; doubleton, 1 point.

entry   A card providing a means to win a trick in a specific hand.

face cards   The three cards in each suit with representations of a court figure: a king, a queen, and a jack.

finesse   An attempt to win a trick with a card when the defenders hold one or more higher-ranking cards in the suit.

first hand   The first player to contribute a card to a trick.

fit   A combined partnership holding of eight or more cards in a suit. An eight-card fit makes a suitable trump suit.

follow suit   Play a card to a trick in the suit that was led. Players must follow suit if they can.

forcing bid   A bid that partner is not expected to pass.

fourth hand   The last of the four players to contribute a card to a trick.

game   A contract with a trick score of 100 or more points: 3NT, 4♥, 4♠, 5♣, or 5♦.

game bonus   The scoring bonus awarded for bidding and making a game contract. The bonus depends on the form of scoring.

grand slam   A contract to take all thirteen tricks: 7♣, 7♦, 7♥, 7♠, or 7NT.

hand   The cards held by one of the players. Also used to refer to the full deal—the hands held by all four players.

high card points (HCPs)   The point-count value given to the high cards in a hand: ace, 4; king, 3; queen, 2; jack, 1.

high cards   The top four cards in each suit: ace, king, queen, and jack.

honors   The five highest-ranked cards in each suit: the ace, king, queen, jack, and ten.

invitational bid   A bid encouraging partner to continue bidding.

joker   An extra card that comes with the deck, not used in the game of bridge.

kibitz   Watch a bridge game. A spectator at a bridge game is called a kibitzer.

length   The number of cards held in a suit; development of a card into a potential winner by removing all cards held by the opponents in the suit.

length points   The value attributed to long suits when valuing a hand using the Point Count Method. 1 point is added for a five-card suit; 2 points for a six-card suit; 3 points for a seven-card suit.

level   The number from one to seven named in a bid during the auction. By adding in the assumed "book" of six tricks, the level indicates the number of tricks to be taken. A bid at the two level would be a contract to take eight (2 + 6) tricks.

limit bid   A bid which describes the strength of the hand within a narrow range of about 3 points. For example, a 1NT opening bid.

limit raise   A raise of partner's suit promising a defined range of strength.

major suit   Hearts or spades.

make   Succeed in taking the number of tricks required to fulfill the contract.

minor suit   Clubs or diamonds.

negative response   An artificial bid used to show a very weak hand. For example, the response of 2NT to an opening strong two-bid.

notrump   A contract with no trump suit. Each trick is won by the highest card played in the suit led.

opener's rebid   Opener's second bid.

opening bidder   The player making the first bid during an auction.

opening lead   The card led to the first trick by the player on declarer's left.

open the bidding Make the first bid during the auction.

opponents The members of the opposite partnership; the defenders from declarer's point of view.

overcall A bid made after the other partnership has opened the bidding.

overtrick A trick taken by declarer beyond the number required to fulfill the contract.

partnership The two players seated opposite each other at the bridge table. North and South are partners; East and West are partners.

partscore A contract with a trick score of fewer than 100 points.

pattern The number of cards held in each suit in a player's hand.

penalty The bonus awarded to the defenders for defeating a contract.

penalty double A double made with the intention of increasing the bonus for defeating the contract.

play The phase of the game following the auction during which the declarer tries to fulfill the contract.

preemptive opening bid An opening bid in a suit at the three level or higher showing a long suit and a weak hand.

promotion Developing a card into a potential winner by driving out any higher-ranking cards held by the opponents.

raise Support partner's suit by bidding the suit at a higher level.

rank The cards within each suit are ranked in order during the play. The ace is the highest, then the queen, jack, ten...down to the two. The suits are ranked in alphabetical order during the auction. Clubs are the lowest, then diamonds, hearts, and spades. Notrump ranks higher than spades.

rebid The second bid made by opener or responder during the auction.

redouble A bid that increases the bonuses for making or defeating the contract after it has already been doubled.

responder The partner of the opening bidder; the partner of a player making an overcall or takeout double.

responder's rebid The second bid made by responder during the auction.

ruffing Playing a trump to a trick when holding no cards in the suit led. Same as trumping.

second hand The second player to contribute a card to a trick.

shape The number of cards held in each suit in a player's hand.

shuffle   Mixing together the cards in the deck prior to the deal.

sign-off bid   A bid which partner is expected to pass.

singleton   A holding of one card in a suit.

small slam   A contract to take twelve tricks: 6♣, 6♦, 6♥, 6♠, or 6NT.

suits   The four groupings of cards within the deck, each character-ized by a symbol: spades (♠), hearts (♥), diamonds (♦), and clubs (♣).

support   The number of cards held in a suit bid by partner; to raise partner's suit to a higher level.

sure trick   A trick which can be taken without giving up the lead to the opponents.

takeout double   A double of an opponent's bid that asks partner to choose another suit as trump.

third hand   The third player to contribute a card to a trick.

trick   The four cards contributed during each round of the play. Starting with the player on lead, each player contributes a card in clockwise rotation. In notrump, the highest-ranking card played in the suit led wins the trick. In a suit contract, a trump played to a trick automatically wins unless a higher trump is played. The player winning a trick leads to the next trick.

trick score   The points scored for bidding and making a contract, not including overtricks. Minor suit contracts are worth 20 points per trick; major suits are worth 30 points per trick; notrump is worth 40 points for the first trick, 30 points per trick thereafter.

trumping   Playing a trump to a trick when holding no cards in the suit led. Same as ruffing.

trump suit   The suit, if any, named in the contract. If one or more trump cards are played on a trick, the highest trump card wins the trick.

unbalanced hand   A hand containing a void, a singleton, or more than one doubleton.

unbid suit   A suit that has not been bid during the auction.

undertrick   Each trick by which declarer's side fails to fulfill the contract.

void   A holding of zero cards in a suit.

vulnerability   Condition under which bonuses and penalties are in-creased. The determination of vulnerability depends on the form of scoring.

winner   A card held by one of the players that will win a trick when it is played.

Scoring

The object of the game is to score points, and this can be done in two ways: *trick score* and *bonus points*. Bridge can be scored using different formats, the three most common being *rubber, duplicate*, and *Chicago*. While the trick score remains the same in all forms of the game, the way the bonuses are awarded can vary. Since rubber bridge scoring is the basis for the other formats, we'll start with that and then discuss the differences in duplicate and Chicago scoring.

Rubber Bridge Scoring

The trick score points are accumulated to produce *games*. The first partnership to win two games wins the *rubber*.

The Score Sheet

The points scored by both sides are recorded on a score sheet which looks like this:

	WE	THEY
Above the line ▶	*500*	*30*
Below the line ▶	*100*	
		120
	80	
	40	
Totals ▶	*720*	*150*

As you might expect, points won by your side go under the "We" column, and points scored by the other side go under the "They" column. The horizontal line about half way down the sheet separates the trick score from the bonuses. Trick scores go below the line; bonuses are entered above the line.

Trick Score

If declarer makes the contract, points are awarded for the **contracted** number of tricks as follows:

Clubs (♣) and diamonds (♦) 20 points per trick.

Hearts (♥) and spades (♠) 30 points per trick.

Notrump   40 points for the first trick and
                            30 points for each subsequent trick.

For example, if you take nine tricks in a contract of 3♥ you get a trick score of 90 points below the line.

Overtricks

If you take ten tricks in your 3♥ contract you still get a trick score of 90 points below the line, but the 30 points for the extra trick—the *overtrick*—are scored as a bonus above the line.

Game

You score a game when you get 100 or more points below the line. This can be done in a single hand, by bidding to a *game contract* worth 100 or more points. 3NT, 4♥, 4♠, 5♣, and 5♦ are the minimum contracts in each denomination that are worth 100 or more points. A contract worth less than 100 points is called a *partscore*. A game can also be scored by accumulating two or more partscores that add up to 100 or more points.

As soon as one side scores a game, a line is drawn on the score sheet below the trick scores. Both sides must start again to accumulate the 100 points needed for a game.

Vulnerability

A side which scores a game is referred to as being *vulnerable*. This has an effect on any subsequent bonus points that are awarded.

Rubber Bonus

The first side to score two games wins the rubber. A bonus of 700 points is awarded if the rubber is won two games to none. A bonus of 500 points is awarded if the rubber is won two games to one.

If you stop playing before a rubber is complete, you get a bonus of 300 points for a game and 100 points for a partscore in an unfinished game.

Slam Bonus

The bonuses awarded for bidding and making a small slam (6♣, 6♦, 6♥, 6♠, or 6NT) or a grand slam (7♣, 7♦, 7♥, 7♠, or 7NT) depend on the vulnerability as follows:

	Nonvulnerable	*Vulnerable*
Small Slam	500	750
Grand Slam	1000	1500

Undertricks

The side that defeats a contract receives a bonus above the line for each trick—*undertrick*—by which the contract was defeated. The bonus depends on the vulnerability as follows:

Nonvulnerable	*Vulnerable*
50 points per undertrick	100 points per undertrick

Doubles and Redoubles

The effect of doubles and redoubles is to increase the scores for making or defeating the contract.

If a doubled contract is made, the trick score below the line is doubled, and a bonus of 50 points is awarded. The bonus for any overtricks depends on the vulnerability as follows:

Nonvulnerable	*Vulnerable*
100 points per overtrick	200 points per overtrick

If a doubled contract is defeated, the defenders' bonus for each undertrick depends on the vulnerability as follows:

Nonvulnerable	*Vulnerable*
100 points for the first undertrick	200 points for the first undertrick
200 points for the second undertrick	300 points for each undertrick thereafter
200 points for the third undertrick	
300 points for each undertrick thereafter	

If a redoubled contract is made, the trick score below the line is multiplied by four, and a bonus of 100 points is awarded. The bonus for any overtricks is twice the doubled bonus.

If a redoubled contract is defeated, the defender's bonus for each undertrick is twice the doubled bonus.

Honors

There are five trump honors, the ace, king, queen, jack, and ten. If one player holds any four of these, the partnership gets a bonus of 100 points. If one player holds all five of the trump honors, the partnership gets a bonus of 150 points. In a notrump contract, a bonus of 150 points is given if one player holds all four aces.

Duplicate Scoring

The primary difference in scoring between duplicate bridge and rubber bridge is that there's no rubber bonus. The vulnerability on each hand in duplicate scoring is predetermined. In place of the rubber bonus, a bonus for making the contract is awarded at the end of each hand based on the vulnerability as follows:

	Nonvulnerable	*Vulnerable*
Partscore contract	50 points	50 points
Game contract	300 points	500 points

The trick score and all other bonuses remain the same, with the exception that there's no bonus for honors in duplicate bridge.

Chicago Scoring

Chicago, or *four-deal bridge*, is an abbreviated form of rubber bridge. Since a rubber of bridge might continue for many hands—until one side scores two games—the Chicago format is used to limit each rubber, or *chukker*, to four deals. At the end of four deals, the players can change partners or move to another table if there are several tables in play.

Chicago is scored in a similar manner to rubber bridge with two exceptions. First, the vulnerability on each of the four deals is determined as follows:

First deal—Both sides nonvulnerable.

Second and third deal—Dealer's side vulnerable, other side nonvulnerable.

Fourth deal—Both sides vulnerable.

If all four players pass, the hand is dealt out again by the same dealer.

The second change is that there's no rubber bonus. Instead, a bonus of 300 points is immediately awarded for making a nonvulnerable game and a bonus of 500 points is awarded for a vulnerable game—similar to duplicate scoring. As in rubber bridge, partscores can be accumulated to score a game. A partnership gets a bonus of 100 points on the fourth deal if it makes a partscore that isn't sufficient to score a game.

This is a good format to use for a party bridge game at home when there are two or more tables of players. There's a break at the end of every fourth hand, which provides lots of opportunity to socialize.

Bi-Monthly Newsletter

Audrey Grant's Better Bridge Newsletter, which keeps you informed on what's happening in the world of bridge today. There are articles on a wide variety of topics including play, defense, bidding conventions, famous hands, bridge etiquette, and bridge history.

For a year's subscription, send $19.95 (U.S. dollars) and your name and mailing address to:

Better Bridge Newsletter
11333 Moorpark St., Suite 458
Studio City, California 91602

Cruises and Seminars

Audrey Grant's Better Bridge Cruises and Tours™, are offered regularly. Details can be obtained from:

Audrey Grant's Better Bridge Cruises and Tours™
Empress Bridge Cruises and Tours
1-800-724-1386; FAX: 607-785-9919

Bridge Supplies

Randy Baron produces a full-color catalog of bridge supplies, including a selection of cards and other specialties. The American Contract Bridge League also has a catalog offering bridge supplies.

Baron-Barclay Bridge Supplies
3600 Chamberlain Lane, Suite 230
Louisville, KY 40241
1-800-274-2221; 502-426-0410; FAX: 502-426-2044

The American Contract Bridge League
Order Department—The Bridge Source
2990 Airways Blvd.
Memphis, TN 38116-3847
1-800-264-2743; FAX: 901-398-7754